Ethics in a Business Society

Charles Seale-Hayne Library
University of Plymouth
(01752) 588 588
LibraryandITenquiries@plymouth.ac.uk

Ethics in a Business Society

By
MARQUIS W. CHILDS
and
DOUGLASS CATER

GREENWOOD PRESS, PUBLISHERS
WESTPORT, CONNECTICUT

Library of Congress Cataloging in Publication Data

Childs, Marquis William, 1903-
    Ethics in a business society.

    Reprint of the ed. published by Harper, New York.
    Includes bibliography.
    1. Christianity and economics. 2. Church and
social problems. 3. Ethics. 4. United States--
Economic policy. I. Cater, Douglass, 1923-   joint
author. II. Title.
HB72.C45 1973   174'.4   73-7073
ISBN 0-8371-6905-4

Originally published in 1954
by Harper & Brothers, New York

Reprinted with the permission
of Harper & Row, Publishers, Inc.

Reprinted in 1973 by Greenwood Press,
a division of Williamhouse-Regency Inc.

Library of Congress Catalogue Card Number 73-7073

ISBN 0-8371-6905-4

Printed in the United States of America

CONTENTS

Foreword

BECAUSE IT SEEMS part of the air we breathe, most of us in America are inclined to take for granted the heritage that has come down to us out of the past two thousand years. We came to this great, rich, beautiful continent and we subdued it by our labors, our daring, our inventiveness, our endurance. And because of our achievement, the vastly productive society we fashioned with our ever-advancing technology, we have felt that we were entitled by right to freedom, to justice; to the rewards of the mind and spirit as well as those of the material world, with its rich profusion constantly set forth before us in the ingenuity of our merchandising system.

This confidence, which to less fortunate nations sometimes looks like smug complacence, was severely jolted by the depression which began in the late 'twenties and continued throughout the 'thirties with more than ten million persons unemployed during most of that period. Something was wrong. We were not sure what it was. Old loyalties and old faiths were shaken.

Although we are at present in the full flush of a prosperity such as even this country has not before experienced, the unquestioning confidence of the past has not been regained. On the contrary, we see on every hand doubt, insecurity, uncertainty. More and more individuals are seeking absolutes as though they could not endure the burden of freedom. They demand certainties, though at the same time they may know that these certainties do violence to the complex reality of the world in which we find ourselves.

Fortunately, however, others have been led by the mounting sense of insecurity and doubt to examine assumptions long taken for granted. With both courage and candor they have set out to examine the past in relation to both the present and the future. What is the base of our faith, our convictions? Has the inheritance out of the past become irrelevant to our present dilemma while we took it complacently for granted? Are the ethical and religious sanctions from the past still valid for our time? Is there any coherence left in the restless, shifting mass of the American people? Do we still hold the view that hard work is bound to bring its reward, or are we bent on shelter under the umbrella of government security? These and an infinite number of other questions occur to each of us in a time when all values seem to be subject to some cosmic solvent. Inevitably the place of religion in man's life has come in for a re-examination, a new and almost wistful scrutiny. More and more individuals in their questing, their searching anxiety, are asking whether religion is relevant to daily life or is something reserved for an hour or an hour and a half once a week; something that is pleasant and consoling, to be taken or left as one may feel the need.

This same concern is deeply felt within the churches. Evidence of it is the series of important studies originated in the Federal Council of Churches with its Department of the Church and Economic Life which was formed in 1947. The Federal Council of Churches in 1950 became a part of the National Council of the Churches of Christ in the U.S.A., an organization made up of twenty-five Protestant and five Greek Orthodox religious bodies of this country whose individual members total some thirty-five million Christians. Meanwhile the Department of the Church and Economic Life had set up a special committee to plan and oversee its study project.

These studies are an inquiry into the relationship between religion and economics, into the department of the spirit and the department of getting and spending; into the easy assumptions that all will be for the best in the best possible of worlds if only each man digs and delves to the best of his own ability.

Financed by one of the great foundations, this was an extraordinary enterprise. Scholars in various fields—economics, sociology, anthropology, psychology, the law—were called in to sit down with theologians, moral philosophers and ministers. From both sides came a critical examination of what each professed. Nothing quite like this effort to relate God to man and man to business had been undertaken before.

Concern over the state of the world had long been a motivating force in the Federal Council of Churches which for several decades antedated the National Council of Churches. But it had been expressed, as Charles P. Taft has put it, pretty much in a spirit of crusading for the underdog. The current studies undertook to supply some answers to the myriad questions troubling not alone the underdog but the top dog; not alone the man at the

vii

bottom of the heap but those on the precarious pinnacle, and practically everyone else in between, since economic insecurity and ethical patterns were seen to be not just a matter of economic levels. The answers could hardly be objective inasmuch as they deal with matters in which opinion and belief are important as well as facts. They were answers by some of the most thoughtful minds of our time deeply and continuously concerned with the dilemma of modern man in his search for certainty, for belief, for faith.

The first of these studies to appear was a symposium called "Goals of Economic Life" (A. Dudley Ward, editor). Under the direction of the Department a group of leading American economists began by discussing their views of society with a biologist, an anthropologist, a psychologist, a lawyer, a philosopher, a political scientist, a sociologist, and two distinguished theologians. The contributions they then prepared for the volume range over the whole field of man's spiritual and intellectual quest in his economic activity. The result is a challenging book which is bound to set the reader off on new paths of examination and discovery.

The second study, by Professor Kenneth Boulding of the University of Michigan, is an analysis of what he calls "the organizational revolution"—the development of a multitude of organizations of increasing scope in many fields of activity. He includes large-scale economic enterprises which have contributed so much to America's productivity. On the whole Professor Boulding expresses a sympathetic view of a system in which many men take many decisions for the common goals of productivity. Professor Reinhold Niebuhr and other critics supply a commentary expressing doubt and skepticism about the techniques of giant organization.

A third study, by Professor Howard R. Bowen of Williams College, is "The Social Responsibility of the Businessman." This is an effort to determine how nearly businessmen do relate their ethics and religion to their daily work. Professor Bowen finds a fairly high level of ethical content entering into the businessman's efforts to solve his day-to-day problems.

"American Income and Its Use" is both statistical and interpretive. Statistics on the distribution of income, on trends in consumption, on changes in family structures, and on various relevant topics are used, against a background of values, in the application of ethics to these aspects of modern life. Professor Elizabeth E. Hoyt of Iowa State College and her collaborators have made this one of the most informing and thought-provoking practical surveys of trends in the everyday life of our people. The book undertakes to determine whether there is a low point at which too little of the world's goods can undermine character and a high point at which too much can destroy it.

The fifth study, "Attitudes and Opinions of People on the American Economy," was prepared under the direction of A. Dudley Ward. It analyzes primarily the different incentives for work. A polling method was used with over five hundred individuals in cooperation with a nationally known public opinion research organization. Also some forty groups were organized including all kinds of people—farm, factory, business, and professional—distributed geographically around the country. Important material was also prepared by psychiatrists on the staff of a university-sponsored study of human relations. Through these various means an effort has been made to find what motives keep men and women usefully employed above the level of survival and what their attitudes are toward their work.

"Christian Values and Economic Life," the sixth volume in the series, has sections by Howard R. Bowen, Professor John C. Bennett of Union Theological Seminary, William Adams Brown, Jr., of the Brookings Institution in Washington, and Bishop G. Bromley Oxnam. Dr. Brown's commentary is especially provocative since it deals with the ethical implications of American economic foreign policy and the responsibility this country has to help other people to raise their standards of living.

A group process was followed throughout the series. The work of each author was subjected to comments and suggestions from consultants and critics (in some cases as many as thirty).

Our volume was originally stimulated by the series itself. During our writing we have had access to both the published volumes and the manuscripts still to be published and other sources. What we have written, therefore, is not a part of the study series itself but rather our interpretation and reflection on all the materials we have used.

We have undertaken to present in as readable a form as

ix

possible some of the results of the churches' effort to relate the seemingly unrelated parts of our society. That means perhaps oversimplification, and in many instances we have been able to do scarcely more than suggest the conclusions of thoughtful and learned men. Many readers will turn to the full-length studies for the penetrating and extended discussions there presented.

But we have tried to make this something other than a summary or a digest of the series. We have sought to put the whole effort, summing up important trends at the midpoint of this extraordinary century, in an historical framework. Looked at in the perspective of history, this point is a kind of milestone. In some respects it may be said to mark the end of an era. Whether it may also be the introduction to a new period in which God, man, and business are more closely interrelated no one can foretell.

Essentially this is a declaration that economics and religion cannot be kept in watertight compartments, as in the recent past many would have separated these elements of man's activity. Inherent in the whole undertaking is a conviction of the relevance of religion and ethics to the decisions that each of us must make as we earn our daily bread.

Acknowledgements

WE HAVE DRAWN on many sources in an effort to give some idea of the range of thought on the central problem of this book. We are, therefore, in the debt of many authors living and dead. We are also indebted to many individuals for invaluable help. Our especial thanks go to A. Dudley Ward, formerly of the Department of the Church and Economic Life of the National Council of Churches in Christ, and to members of the Department's staff. We have received unfailing help and cooperation from the staff of the Library of Congress. For research and for advice and encouragement we are deeply indebted to both of our wives. The patient and painstaking assistance of Mrs. H. B. Hood has made the preparation of the manuscript possible in spite of a deadline all too quickly upon us. We ourselves are, of course, responsible for any errors of fact or interpretation.

CHAPTER I

The Age of Certitude

THE SUGGESTION that religion was in any sense irrelevant to the immediate concerns of daily life would have seemed strange in the Middle Ages. Such a suggestion might even have sounded heretical in an age when the embrace of the Church included man's every thought and action. We are so much the children of our time, the result of the long process of rationalizing, liberalizing thought, of Reason applied to Nature, progressing from Hume and Locke to Jefferson and the pragmatism of the American outlook, that it is difficult for us to comprehend that earlier era when men lived so largely within a closed circle described by the Church and its canons.

In the Middle Ages the primary concern of rich and poor alike, the feudal lord and the peasant-serf, was the salvation of the soul. Man's time on earth was brief and for the most part filled with trials and tribulations. He expected little else in the short interlude before eternity. By the beginning of the fourteenth century the Schoolmen had prepared a comprehensive body of theological law covering every phase of life.

The economic life of the time, certainly in the initial phase, was on a narrow and restricted basis. And even as the beginnings of a more extensive commerce appeared,

11

the ethical dictates of the Church were a widely influential force. As R. H. Tawney puts it in his brilliant and erudite "Religion and the Rise of Capitalism":

"Hence all activities fall within a single system, because all, though with different degrees of immediateness, are related to a single end, and derive their significance from it. The Church in its wider sense is the Christian Commonwealth, within which that end is to be realized; in its narrower sense it is the hierarchy divinely commissioned for its interpretation; in both it embraces the whole of life, and its authority is final. Though practice is perpetually at variance with theory, there is no absolute division between the inner and personal life, which is 'the sphere of religion,' and the practical interests, the external order, the impersonal mechanism, to which, if some modern teachers may be trusted, religion is irrelevant."

Usury was a sin. Trade itself was dubious in the ethical view of the Church. As one authority expressed it, "whosoever buys a thing, not that he may sell it whole and unchanged, but that it may be a material for fashioning something, he is no merchant. But the man who buys it in order that he may gain by selling it again unchanged and as he bought it, that man is of the buyers and sellers who are cast forth from God's temple." This was the view of the master theologian, St. Thomas Aquinas, and it was expressed in even sharper terms by St. Antoninus, a specialist in the economic life of the Middle Ages. Because trade and usury were considered sinful, these functions, as the sluggish current of commerce began to quicken a little, were left largely to those outside the Church whose souls, in the view of the time, could not be further jeopardized.

Through the intervening centuries a complete reversal

has taken place. Acquisition, increase of money, mercantile achievement, considered in the Middle Ages vices comparable to lust and gluttony, became in the era of capitalism major virtues.

The society of the Middle Ages was, of course, a static society, based largely on an agricultural economy. It was a poor society in which, while the extremes of power and wealth, as between the feudal lord and serf, were great, the total supply of goods from outside the manors was limited to what the few guilds and traders could furnish. There was, it is scarcely necessary to say, no understanding of commerce and trade in the sense they have come to have in our time.

In this poor society even if all the incomes had been made equal the poverty of the poor would scarcely have been relieved one whit. As Professor Boulding points out in "Goals of Economic Life," we have learned in our time that the increase of productivity is a precondition to the abolition of poverty. Such a concept was wholly alien to the Middle Ages. Under the hierarchical system of that era prices were to be established at such a level, preferably by official action, that each man would "have the necessaries of life suitable for his station." In the ban on usury, Tawney points out, the emphasis was on taking a payment for money which was fixed and certain as between borrower and lender. The crime was in the kind of pact specifying that the usurer should get his money back with an increase whether the borrower gained or lost.

But while every man was fixed in his station from lowest to highest, they were all enclosed within the same carefully defined circle of values. Under the eye of God, to the end of the salvation of the soul, they were the same even though the peasant was little better than a slave working out his tribute to the lord of the manor. But the powers of the lord of the manor were after all only earthly powers.

Within the unity of the Church all kinds and classes were one, and it was the continuing concern of the Church to protect the humble and the helpless from the rich and avaricious. Those guilty of avarice were made to do penance by giving large alms. Punishment was meted out not only to usurers for taking what we would now call interest, but to those who were able to buy cheaper and with the passage of time to sell dearer. In practice, of course, at one level and another these canons were violated. There remained nevertheless into the late Middle Ages, when the rising tide of trade from city to city was breaking down the old barriers, the fundamental belief of priests and people alike that traffic in money and goods endangered the soul.

Looking back from our own time of confusion to this era when the walls of faith encompassed man's every act whether mean or noble, we undoubtedly exaggerate the sense of oneness that this brought. Yet the great cathedrals could scarcely have risen had they not come out of a common devotion to the glory of God. With their infinity of detail, their imaginativeness, the evidence of devotion and dedication in craftsmanship and artistry, they could not have been ordered into being, as were the pyramids, by a despot.

Romanticized as this epoch has been, one may nevertheless see in the cathedrals proof of rewards and satisfactions in a way of life that had this magnificent flowering. Here was the visible sign of men's love of God made manifest. That the cathedrals should have been the supreme achievement of a Christian society was no accident. Nor was it any happenstance that artisans and craftsmen from the whole country round contributed their labors through months and years to the common purpose of a community inseparably bound together.

In "Goals of Economic Life," Eduard Heimann, Professor of Economics in the New School for Social Research and lecturer on Christian Ethics in the Union Theological Seminary, points up in forceful and moving language the contrasting fragmentation of our own time. He speaks of the two "rationalist systems," the individualist and the collectivist. Both, says Professor Heimann, miss the unity of person and community. The individualist system misses it by making the strong individual supreme and making "society a derived value, a means for ends of individual welfare." A collectivist system treats the individual as a means to be used or destroyed as expedience suggests to the end of a theoretical perfection. Then Professor Heimann adds:

"What makes the individual a person and the collective a community is the power of love, which transcends the cleavage and possible conflict between them by creating the person as a loving and loved person and the community as a community of persons rather than of atoms. This fundamental Christian proposition has no place in the logic of either one of the rationalist systems."

While in Professor Heimann's view both systems are "anti-Christian," he points out that rational individualism—despite the French Revolution—implies toleration while collectivism repudiates it. Individualism does not inquire into motives but regards them as strictly private and tolerates, among others, Christian motives. Then in a noteworthy passage he suggests that whatever of unity is left to us can be attributed to the power of social cohesion "sustained for generations and centuries by the long-surviving unofficial inheritance of Christian morality, which is precisely what gave rationalism the illusion that people can live without religion. Now that the danger of final disintegration looms large," he adds, "the attempt is made to draw upon Christian moral reserves for reintegration of capitalism by equating Christianity with laissez faire, and the sermon on losing one's soul in order to save it with the doctrine of the 'supreme value of the individual' in search of 'self-realization.' "

We can readily understand, therefore, why so many people have for so many reasons during the past century or more looked back with something like longing to that earlier time. Then all men seemed to share a common destiny within the golden circle of the will of God. With the crude clang and clash of the onrush of the industrial revolution and all the ugliness that it brought in its wake, sensitive souls in mid-nineteenth-century England tried to find their way back to what seemed across the centuries an age of divinely appointed certitude. There was even a conscious effort through something resembling the guild system to revive the skills of the craftsman and his joy in fashioning with his hands objects of enduring beauty. This same nostalgia for a past that called upon a man's whole being, his soul and his heart as well as his mind and his ambition, was felt occasionally in America where almost everyone was preoccupied with making his own way as part of the enormous task of conquering a continent.

One of the interesting figures at the turn of the century was the shy and lonely semi-recluse Henry Adams. Descended from the New England family that had contributed so much to America's greatness, Adams was repelled by the insistent commercialism, the materialism that he saw all around him. He spent much of his time in Europe, submerging himself for long periods in a study of the cathedrals of France and of the men who built them.

One result was Adams' remarkable book "Mont St. Michel and Chartres" which is such a curious combination of scholarship, snobbism, and a tragic longing for an age forever gone. That book had something to do with the revival of Gothic architecture in city churches and on college campuses throughout America as architecture tended to become archeology. The vaulted roof, the spire, the gargoyle were reproduced wholesale in a land that had been empty wilderness when the cathedrals were built. But it was symptomatic above all of a nostalgia which has led many in subsequent years to look back to the medieval church as though the spirit of a common purposiveness, a common acceptance, could be reproduced in similar fashion in a time so far removed and so completely different.

While the haze of the passing centuries may distort our vision, the Church in the Middle Ages seemed to bring men together with a sense of brotherhood that we seek in vain in the world today. This search is a theme running through many of the essays in "Goals of Economic Life."

We find Alfred E. Emerson, Professor of Zoology at the University of Chicago, in his discussion of the biological foundations of ethics and social progress, stating that the concept of the "brotherhood" of all mankind rests upon "firm biological principles." As we shall see later, from this belief derives the widely held conviction that the natural evolution of human society is an extension or an outgrowth of the evolution of biological species including man. This concept had a profound influence on the thought of the nineteenth century. Professor Emerson in the following statement expresses both the bold assumption and the uncertainty of the social scientist today:

> "It is not possible to predict with certitude that a social evolution away from national conflict and devastating war will occur within a decade or so. It may take many centuries to achieve. In the meantime it may be necessary to operate on the cancers in the body politic that seem to rise and flourish temporarily to the detriment of both the diseased and the healthy parts of the human supra-organism. At present there

is too little social science that diagnoses social disease
and discovers cures. . . ."

In his "Anthropological View of Economics" Professor
Ralph Linton of Yale University recognizes that the extreme stress on individualism in our time, and the conse-
quent uprootedness and mobility to which rapid technological change has contributed, results in a breakdown
of the close and continuing social ties coming out of the
past. As Professor Linton points out, a considerable part
of the modern industrial population in our age passes its
life without any real roots and therefore with both the
freedom for individual choice and the psychological insecurity which this condition means. Inevitably the values
of power and prestige come to take precedence over all
others. And the symbols of prestige tend to reduce themselves to such obvious tokens as mink coats and shiny
automobiles. Yet Professor Linton is sufficiently optimistic
to believe that in view of what we know of human behavior in general it is highly probable that the present phase
of social disintegration is transitory.

In his study of the psychological basis of human values
Donald Snygg, Professor of Psychology at State University
Teachers College, Oswego, New York, finds that the greatest obstacle in the way of universal brotherhood at the
present time is not man's unregenerate selfishness and individualism. It is the fact that to give their lives meaning
and dignity the people of the world have identified themselves with a great number of conflicting groups and
causes for which many of them are prepared to sacrifice
themselves and others. That is another way of saying we
live in a world of fragments and factions forever splitting
off and warring one against the other. When it comes to
incentives the desire of the American industrial worker
for group membership and approval usually proves more
potent than the desire for money when the two are in

conflict. Professor Snygg believes, too, that we do not stress nearly enough the motive of service inherent in our society as against the motive of greed.

John C. Bennett, Professor of Christian Theology and Ethics at Union Theological Seminary, in his chapter, "Theological Conception of Goals for Economic Life," holds that all of life must be the province of man's fate. In a sense Professor Bennett can be said to bring a cycle to a close. As an advocate of the social gospel, he believes that the church has a direct interest in the whole welfare of each individual. He holds that man cannot serve mammon six days a week and God on the seventh. He rejects the comfortable assumption that if only we do not interfere with economic forces they will bring about an automatic adjustment resulting in the greatest good for the greatest number. In a notable passage in this chapter of "Goals of Economic Life" Professor Bennett expresses as well as anyone in the entire series the modern view of the relation of the whole man to religion:

"The Christian can put what has happened within the Church in terms of the following change of thought: It is not enough to say that economic processes in themselves reveal God's purpose for economic life; we must bring to economic life what we know of God's purpose for the whole of human life as it is known to us in Christ. The Christian must reject as a deadly heresy the idea of two absolutely different standards, one for the Kingdom of God or the Church or the personal relations of men, and another for the economic order. God as known in Christ is the Lord of all life."

Yet Professor Bennett recognizes that the efforts of the medieval church to regulate in detail all economic life brought about a justifiable rebellion. Once a new vitality,

a new inventiveness, began to thrust up into the static
society of the Middle Ages, the narrow laws, imposed with
the sanction of the Church, had a stifling effect. Those
tight restrictions seemed to men to stand in the way of the
new vista of plenty suddenly opening out beyond the
walls that had for so long encompassed all of life.

To many the old way had begun to seem a harsh existence, as indeed it was, a large part of the population living at almost an animal level. Gautier de Coincy in the
thirteenth century pictured the peasant, poor, sad, and
downcast with little bread and an evil couch. His lot is
hard, he works from morning to night. Yet he can hardly
be said to deserve more since too often he forgets God and
works on Sundays or Holy Days. His cottage is of mud
and timber, rising little above the ground and covered
with straw. Here is the peasant in that elementary society:

"They are ever an unquiet crew, laborious and un-
clean. They bring to the nearest town whatsoever
each has gained either from his field or from the
produce of his flock; and here they buy in return
whatsoever each needeth; for they have few or no
artificers dwelling among them. On Holy Days they
come all together in the morning to the church
whereof there is commonly one for each village; there
they hear from their priest God's word and the sacrament (sacra) ; then, after noon, they treat of their
own affairs under a linden tree or in some other public place. After this, the younger folks dance to the
sound of the pipe, while the olders go to the tavern
and drink wine. None goeth unarmed in public; each
has his sword by his side for any chance emergency."

Ever more frequent wars ravaged the countryside.
Repeated drafts to meet the crusades emptied the villages
of husbandmen. Again and again the miserable people at

the bottom of the heap revolted, but the end was almost always greater repression.

It was a medieval tenet that class divisions were of God's making. Even the best churchmen were far less often concerned with actually improving the status of the poor than with preaching contentment in poverty. Differences between serf and lord were settled in the manor court where the lord of the manor was as often as not both party to the case and judge, although in theory he was an impartial arbiter. The lord of the manor had lawyers who could define the position of the serf as, for instance, a man who "ought not know in the evening what work might be demanded of him tomorrow and is always liable to uncertain duties and may be tallaged at the will of his lord, more or less, and must give blood-money for leave to give his daughter in marriage."

Although ecclesiastical landlords were often no less harsh in exploiting their peasants than were the lords of the manor, many authorities ascribe to the Church a softening influence, contributing to the disappearance of slavery, and the suppression or modification of serfdom. But as the forces of change began to ferment within this closed society, the unity that had held it together seemed to be more and more a matter of compulsion applied from above.

In the French Revolution it was said, "Be my brother, or I kill thee!" This same intransigence, in the view of one historian of the Middle Ages, was applied in the later phase of that era as, "Be at unity with me, or be burned!" Every child was baptized into the Church, or if baptism were willfully omitted, there was presumption of heresy against the parents. All nonconformity was heresy and willful nonconformity was punishable with the stake.

The monopoly claimed by the Church in every department of life came more and more to gall as corruption spread within the Church itself. The rank abuse of the systems of indulgences and the powers of the Papacy caused wide disaffection. Everywhere the seeds of rebellion were taking root.

Above all, the currents of trade, inventiveness, discovery were forcing new channels of thought and conduct. The Portuguese navigators were sailing right out of the tight little world circumscribed for so long by the theologians. The Church was finding it increasingly difficult to enforce the concept of a "just price" on a pattern of trade expanding across medieval boundaries. As the geographical area of markets expanded, it became more and more difficult to fix prices for the necessities of life. The static—stagnant might be a better word—economy that had heretofore been only one compliant department of the Christian commonwealth was in process of swift transformation.

Yet even as these far-reaching changes were beginning to shake the solid, compact structure of the Middle Ages, the powers that be were insisting that nothing could alter the old values; they were reasserting the precepts of the past even as altered conditions made those precepts seem like the irrelevant taboos of a vanished age. Tawney points out that in 1552, with the Scottish Reformation only eight years off, the Catechism of the Archbishop of St. Andrews nevertheless showed no disposition to compromise with the commercial practices then coming into being. That catechism denounced usurers, masters who withhold wages, covetous merchants who sell fraudulent wares, covetous landlords who grind their tenants, and "all wretches that will be grown rich incontinent" as well as "all who may keep their neighbor from poverty and mischance and do it not."

But the dykes constructed out of rule and law and custom, all united by the churchly cement, could not hold back the flood. In less than two generations a revolution in trade and commerce took place that was no less shattering than the industrial revolution of two centuries later. This was a revolution of accumulating capital, a revolution of prices shattering all customary and familiar relationships. Great trading houses such as that of the Fuggers spread their operations over all of Europe. The cities such as Venice that had been so powerful began to yield to the rising power of the new states. The economic imperialism of Spain and Portugal thrust invaders out into continents—Africa, India, the Americas—which had been a dark void until a few years before.

In this revolutionary change sweeping across the world there was a tremendous excitement. The Renaissance contributed to the great onrushing upheaval. The bonds that had held men's minds in a narrow orbit were being shattered. The science and the philosophy of the Greeks had been rediscovered, and the clear light from that distant time helped to brighten the transcending glow in the sky.

Yet it is supremely important to remember that some of the most passionate advocates of change were at the same time insisting that the fundamental canons out of the past must be preserved intact. While Martin Luther's thunderous knock on the door of the old order did as much as anything else to break up the pattern, Luther, as Tawney points out, accepted the social hierarchy with its principles of status and subordination. What he did was knock out a principal foundation of authority. The demand of the peasants that serfdom should end shocked Luther. As he said, "This article would make all men equal and so change the spiritual Kingdom of Christ into an external worldly one. Impossible! An earthly kingdom cannot exist without inequality of persons. Some must be free, others serfs, some rulers, others subjects. As St. Paul says, 'Before Christ both master and slave are one.' "

Luther resisted just as stoutly the concessions that were being made in response to the demands of the new commerce spreading across Europe. He denounced the can-

onists who sought to adjust to the practical necessities of
the time. "The greatest misfortune of the German nation
is easily the traffic in interest," Luther said. "The devil
invented it and the Pope, by giving his sanction to it,
has done untold evil throughout the world." He would
refuse usurers the sacrament, absolution, and Christian
burial. "Foreign merchandise," said this iron reformer,
"which brings from Calicut and India and the like places
wares such as precious silver and jewels and spices . . . and
drains the land and people of their money, should not be
permitted. . . . "

This is important to remember because we have been
so little aware of how much was carried over from the
medieval past into the new age. The religious and ethical
inheritance out of this earlier time has played a part
which modern men have either not understood or have
been unwilling to acknowledge. From the perspective of
the perilous moment in which we live, the premises out of
our long past have been too readily taken for granted.

One may not be sure that those premises are any longer
valid in a society that has undergone such a complete
revolution. We have casually taken for granted the foundation of our social structure when in fact it appears to
have suffered serious erosion. This erosion may explain
the breakdown of values as it helps to explain modern
man's insecurity and his frantic haste to seek a new absolute in the total power of the state.

Such fundamental questions are raised in this connection as we shall continue to ignore at our own mortal
peril. We must never forget that the most monstrous crime
in recorded history took place scarcely a decade ago when,
in what had been one of the most civilized states of the
West, hundreds of thousands, if not millions, of human
beings were murdered not in passion or in war but in the
arrogant pride—madness, if one is charitable—of a theory
stated in cold blood. That is reason enough to examine

the sanctions that underlie, if they do in reality underlie, this insecure society in which we live.

Certainly, too, it is time to reconsider our debt to the past in relation to the strength, or lack of it, of the underpinnings of this swiftly rushing mechanized world in which we find ourselves. The break with the medieval past became so complete with the passage of the years, the reactions against its narrow bounds were so violent, that we may have lost sight of the true meaning of the ties that link the thirteenth century and the twentieth century. Or, it might be well to add, the ties that we assume still to exist. Merely to know and in a small way to understand our heritage from that earlier civilization is important. That is one of the great contributions made by Tawney in his milestone of a book "Religion and the Rise of Capitalism." In a magnificent passage he sums up perhaps as well as can be done the contribution of that time and the contrasting values which we are now beginning to see in a sharper light.

"The significance of its contribution," Tawney says of medieval thought, "consists, not in its particular theories as to prices and interest, which recur in all ages, whenever the circumstances of the economic environment expose consumer and borrower to extortion, but in its insistence that society is a spiritual organism, not an economic machine, and that economic activity, which is one subordinate element within a vast and complex unity, requires to be controlled and repressed by reference to the moral ends for which it supplies the material means. So merciless is the tyranny of economic appetites, so prone to self-aggrandizement the empire of economic interests, that a doctrine which confines them to their proper sphere, as the servant, not the master, of civilization, may reasonably be regarded as among the pregnant truisms which are a permanent element in any sane philosophy. Nor is it, perhaps, as clear today as it seemed a century ago, that it has been an unmixed gain to substitute the criterion of economic expediency, so easily interpreted in terms of quantity and mass, for the conception of a rule of life superior to individual desires and temporary exigencies, which was what the medieval theorist meant by 'natural law.' "

Our individualisms, our freedoms, the rights which we presume almost as we do the sun's coming up in the morning, did not spring full-blown from the rock on which the Pilgrims are said to have landed at Plymouth. Nor did those great men at Philadelphia invent the doctrine so nobly expressed in the Declaration of Independence. They were the inheritors, as are we, of a tradition with roots going far back beyond our limited vision. To know what has come to us out of that tradition is to understand more about the strengths and the weaknesses of our own time. It will help us to know, too, what out of that tradition is vital and meaningful in terms of our own survival in a time of troubles, to use Professor Toynbee's phrase, of a magnitude for which history has no parallel. For one thing, thanks to the technology of our mass communication and mass travel, this time of troubles is world-wide and for the first time, thanks to both the fission and the fusion of the atom in the ordinary atomic bomb and now in the hydrogen bomb, man has the power to destroy all life on this planet.

CHAPTER II

The Circle Is Shattered

THE REVOLUTION that took place in Church and State was
above all a revolution in values. Black became white and
white became black. The reversal is seen most significantly in the phrase "natural law." As the revolution ran its
course that expression came to mean something entirely
different from what it had meant in the Middle Ages. It is
a key to the changing times.

In his contribution to "Goals of Economic Life" Frank
H. Knight, Professor of Social Sciences and Philosophy at
the University of Chicago, discusses this revolution in
values. Dr. Knight finds the society of the Middle Ages the
antithesis of the liberal culture in which American capitalism has developed. Here it is time to say that in this
book we will use the word "liberal" to mean the absence
of restrictions by church and government on the economic
life. For a rationalist like Dr. Knight the Middle Ages was
a "spiritual despotism" in which salvation was prescribed
by the doctrine and ritual carried out from birth and intended to prevent the dogma from being questioned by
impious and presumptuous intellect.

When this did not work, as in the case of eccentric or
obdurate individuals, resort was had to torture and execu-
tion by torture. Yet there is the paradox, as Dr. Knight

makes clear, that out of this system came the only liberal culture known to history. It came through a revolution, a ground swell, that is only partly explained by the swift surface changes taking place. From the East, from Byzantium, from the Moslem world, came new streams of thought and inquiry. The mathematics of the Arab world was the basis of modern science, technology, and business. Perhaps the most immediately potent factor was the lens which opened the way to astronomical discoveries that refuted the neat little maps of the universe drawn up within the frame of the dogma of the Church. Galileo challenged the cosmology of the Schoolmen, and his trial as a heretic is one of the great landmarks in the evolution of freedom of inquiry.

A vast ferment was at work in every department of life. It was not alone impersonal forces that were bringing about revolutionary change but men, zealous, ardent, intensely dedicated, who were figuratively, if not literally, moving heaven and earth. They were intent on reforming not the Church alone but the daily lives of Christians in a new and reformed church.

One of the principal figures in this revolution was John Calvin. As a student in France Calvin prepared himself for the great role that he was to play. The new learning was rapidly supplanting medieval scholasticism. Yet more than a decade after Luther had published his thesis there was in France still no open challenge to the Church of Rome. Then in 1534 when he was twenty-five years old Calvin broke with the power that had for so long held Europe in a kind of unity.

It is hard for us in our time of indifferent choice and swift change to understand what this must have meant to a man of dedicated faith. At Poitiers in a grotto near the town Calvin celebrated for the first time the Communion of the Evangelical Church of France using a rock for a Communion table. Then a year later he published his "The Institutes of the Christian Religion." This contained the complete outline of the Calvinist theological system. Later editions were largely emendation or expansion. At the age of twenty-eight Calvin settled in Geneva and began the development of the stern theocratic society that assumed that every member of the state was also under the discipline of the Church.

The right to exercise this discipline was vested exclusively in the consistory or the body of preachers and elders. The theological system of Calvin prescribed the daily life of man nearly as completely as had the church of the Middle Ages. The rules of daily life were to be sternly and strictly enforced. This from the very start was the essence of Calvinism. In a letter to the Duke of Somerset in October of 1548 Calvin rebuked the English, saying that while crimes of violence were punished the licentious were spared. And the licentious in the view of this intensely devoted man could have no part in the Kingdom of God. In Professor Tawney's phrase, he made Geneva a city of glass in which every household lived its life under the supervision of a spiritual police. The consistory excommunicated drunkards, dancers, and scorners of religion. Punishment was carried out by the Council of Geneva with fines and imprisonment for the dissolute and death for the heretics. Thus there came into being in the city by the Lake of Geneva what a later divine was to call "the most perfect school of Christ that ever was on earth since the days of the Apostles."

Inasmuch as the whole of man was its province, this school naturally concerned itself with the regulation and control of the economic life. "No member (of the Christian body)," Calvin had written in his Institutes, "holds his gifts to himself or for his private use but shares them among his fellow members, nor does he derive benefits save from those things which proceed from the common profit of the body as a whole. Thus the pious man owes to his brethren all that it is in his power to give." The consistory censured harsh creditors. It punished usurers, engrossers, and monopolists. Merchants who defrauded their clients and cloth makers whose stock was an inch too narrow were reprimanded or fined.

In Puritan New England the Calvinist theocratic system was carried to an even more iron extreme than in the reformed community of Geneva. The Puritan fathers sternly set their faces not only against licentiousness, tobacco, immodest fashions and costly apparel, but also against the snares of commerce that lay in wait for true believers. In the wealth of this new Eden Governor Bradford was fearful that material prosperity would be "the ruin of New England, at least of the churches of God there." Tawney credits as the organizer of the first American monopoly the Puritan who owned the only cow on board the Mayflower and sold the milk at two pence a quart. This wicked monopolist was forced to listen to a sermon on the subject of oppression.

The authorities in the Massachusetts Colony regulated prices, limited the rate of interest, fixed a maximum wage, and whipped incorrigible idlers. The price of cattle was to be determined not by the needs of the buyer but at a standard that would yield no more than a reasonable return to the seller. A shopkeeper in Boston charged with profiteering was fined £200. Summoned to church, he "did with tears acknowledge and bewail his covetous and corrupt heart." Tradesmen argued that if they did not make up for the loss on one article by a profit on another, they could not live. But this brought a lengthy sermon setting forth a series of principles and a set of specific rules which were to govern trading.

Yet despite the sternness of the Calvinist rule, the demands of the new commerce were effecting changes in the attitudes of even the most devout. In the rise and fall of the value of money from one corner of Europe to the other, in the balancing off of exports and imports, in the fluctuations caused by speculators, the trader, even though he were a part of the Calvinist system, was faced with reality and not a theory. With indignation the elders at Geneva saw that some of their laws were being breached. Inherent in the Calvinist approach was a new element. To compress it is to risk oversimplification. But the new outlook implied a kind of perfection here on earth. The individual, weak and sinful though he was, must exert himself to the utmost to fulfill his role in a society that tolerated no transgressions. With the passage of time the individual came to believe that his exertions in industry and trade, in laying up wealth, in acquiring goods for himself and his family were part of the virtuous pattern of the righteous man. These hallowed exertions increased not only the account at the bank but the account in heaven. The necessities of daily life became in themselves a part of the plan for perfection. The vulgarization of the doctrine of Calvin was gradually to underwrite the motivations of a developing and expanding capitalism. This is one chapter in the human pattern of self-righteousness.

Predestination was at the center of the Calvinist system. Professor Bennett calls it the most thoroughgoing assertion of the divine sovereignty that we know. Yet, as he points out, it conceded something to human responsibility, for Calvin, somewhat inconsistently, emphasized the idea that man is the author of his own sin. God who causes "the wrath of man to praise Him" overrules man's very disobedience and uses it for his own purposes. What Calvin had done was to shake further the dominion of the Church of Rome. This coincided with the revolutionary upset of a new way of life.

Rules and restrictions embedded in the Calvinist theocracy could not keep the trade of either the old world or the new in bounds. An energetic people had set out on the conquest of the American continent with its fabulous wealth. They were not to be stopped by the civil authority of a royal sovereign in distant London who exercised his power in capricious and arbitrary fashion. And the dictates of the church were being weakened by the exigencies of a commerce that was forever expanding. The rich merchants of New England began to be looked up to. God had meant for his children to prosper in the New World. He had set them down on a shore on which nature was bountifully designed to engineer the Kingdom of Heaven on earth.

Attitudes were undergoing a subtle change. It could be taken that God meant a man to increase his worldly goods for the greater glorification of God and, incidentally, of himself. There were, of course, at the same time many who preached sacrifice, self-denial, and other-worldliness. The Quakers and similar sects renounced all outward manifestations of worldly well-being and success. Holy living and holy dying and the perpetual pains of hell-fire for transgressors were still widely preached.

But the pull of the ships that came and went in the rapidly growing ports of Boston, New York, and Philadelphia, the demands of commerce, with the fertilization of constant drafts of new capital from abroad, were altering habit and custom. They were creating a new society. While it was grown from the Calvinist seed, the fruit it was beginning to bear would have outraged the prophet and lawgiver of Geneva. In the minds of leading men in this intensely practical, intensely industrious society a new rationale was coming into being. It would justify all the works of men (and some of them were strange works indeed such as the traffic in human slavery) to the will of God. That will had become remarkably compliant as the works of men had grown increasingly more complex and ever more demanding on the energy and devotion of man.

The time was ripe for a new philosopher who would articulate men's changing beliefs. One need not be a cynic to suggest that philosophy often seems the handmaiden ready to provide a beautiful prospectus for a house of habit and custom in which society has long since been comfortably adjusting its goods and chattels.

Certainly the way had been well prepared. Calvin's Puritan inheritors had spread the notion that success is not merely a reward for good conduct but the sign and symbol of the virtuous man. "No question," wrote a Puritan pamphleteer, "but it (riches) should be the portion rather of the godly than of the wicked, were it good for them; for godliness has the promises of this life as well as the life to come." In its ultimate vulgarization, "God helps those who help themselves." ,

Adam Smith spent five years writing his "An Inquiry into the Wealth of Nations." It was published by one of those wonderful coincidences of history in the year 1776. In the nearly two centuries that have followed its influence has been incalculable. One must add, in the interest of accuracy, that it is not so much the influence of the book itself as of the popularization of the broad concept taken out of "The Wealth of Nations." It has come to have an almost mythical connotation which takes it clear out of the realm of the economist and into politics at the level at which most of us repeat phrases without knowing very much about what they mean or where they came from. To hear the President of the United States in the year 1953 talk at a press conference, in reply to a question on social security, about that man Adam Smith and what he did or did not mean with respect to the system under which we live is to get some idea of the long shadow cast by the Scottish philosopher who wrote the five volumes of a work that has become a milestone in the history of ideas.

Born in 1723 of parents in modest circumstances who nevertheless gave him all the education they could, Adam Smith as man of letters caused no great stir in the world up until the publication of his magnum opus. On its publication his contemporaries were not slow to recognize its significance. Hume, older and with a far greater reputation, had been hoping, with a touch of Scottish chauvinism perhaps, for much from the younger author whom he considered a kind of protégé. When the book was off the presses, he quickly read through it and then sat down and wrote his friend:

> "Euge! Belle! Dear Mr. Smith, I am much pleased with your performance, and the perusal of it has taken from me a state of great anxiety. It was a work of so much expectation, by yourself, by your friends, and by the public that I trembled for its appearance but am now much relieved. Not but that the reading of it requires so much attention, and the public is so disposed to give so little, that I shall still doubt for some time of its being at first very popular, but it has depth, and solidity, and acuteness, and is so much illustrated by curious facts that it must at last attract the public attention."

In the first volume Adam Smith expounds his basic economic philosophy, a philosophy that was new and stirring and that was to become the great symphonic theme of the industrial revolution and mass production. This in its essence was the theory that the improvement in the productiveness of labor depends largely on the division of labor. Economists consider this an unrivaled exposition of a thesis that has conditioned the lives of men everywhere. Adam Smith shows how this theory applies in much greater force to manufacture than to agriculture and in consequence agriculture relatively must lag behind in the course of economic development. This is as true for our time as it was when it was first expounded.

Adam Smith laid down another fundamental principle. Before the efficient division of labor can be carried out, capital must be accumulated. That stone too went neatly into place in the growing foundation of capitalism. Similarly his new theory of price was basic to the developing structure on which such a towering edifice was to be raised. Not labor alone, in Adam Smith's theory, but wages, profit, and rent all go into making up price.

Adam Smith was not nearly so absolute and arbitrary as some of his latter-day apostles have been. As has happened so often, the prophet's words have been taken out of context and interpreted with a finality that would have shocked and startled their author. He made many concessions to the need for inhibitions whether imposed from within or without. Yet his ardent followers have taken out of context such phrases as "the unseen hand" which automatically in the view of Adam Smith guides the economic process to the end of the greatest good for the greatest number. They have set up such fragments as the ultimate word on the relationship between government and business. One of the present-day apostles of Adam Smith, who owns several newspapers in which he propagandizes his viewpoint, would abolish not only the public schools and the postal system but organized churches, since the churches by their very organization transgress the law of individual dissociation.

Ever since its publication "The Wealth of Nations" has been endlessly interpreted and discussed. Not only the popularizers who pluck out of it what they want, but whole schools of economists have debated it pro and con. It has been in a sense the Bible of the classical school of liberal economists. That great nineteenth-century libertarian, John Stuart Mill, owed a heavy debt to Adam Smith. It may be said in fact that Mill did little more than to elaborate, with his own rhetorical embellishments, on the momentous book that appeared in the momentous year of 1776.

In view of all this, the various specialists brought together in the current study to consider the problem of the

ethical responsibility of the businessmen have naturally
given a great deal of thought to Adam Smith and his influence. In general they are agreed that the economic philosophy which he first articulated and which has since been
so industriously expounded contributed mightily to cast-
ing off the restraints that had held the economic life of the
Middle Ages in a narrow circle. But an economist, a philosopher, a jurist, and a political scientist could hardly be
expected to agree that the influence has been wholly good.
The discussion of Adam Smith that runs through
"Goals of Economic Life" touches many phases of the
organization of society, past and present. Professor Boulding is on the whole a champion of Smith and his economic
philosophy. There is a direct relationship between that
philosophy and the astonishingly successful development
of capitalism in America. Above all it is the freedom of
choice inherent in Adam Smith that has helped to underwrite a strong pluralistic economy. This is directly contrary to the "spirit of orthodoxy" which is the greatest
enemy of change.

In order to suggest how greatly specialization has contributed to economic progress Professor Boulding asks
us to imagine a world of Swiss Family Robinsons. Each
family on its own five acres of land forbidden to trade
with any other family would have to raise its own food,
weave its own cloth, build its own houses, paint its own
pictures, and write its own books. The material and cultural poverty of that kind of world would be beyond
measure, comparable to the poverty of a primitive society.
Without specialization trade would be useless and without trade specialization would be absurd.

"Another theorem regarding economic progress which
also dates back to Adam Smith," Professor Boulding
writes, "is that economic progress almost invariably requires the 'accumulation of stock.' If we extend the concept of accumulation to include the accumulation of

knowledge and skills in the minds and muscles of men, the proposition is incontrovertible. The 'better ways of doing things' which economic progress implies nearly always involve the use of more elaborate and costly implements; and so especially in poor societies the difficulty of accumulation may be the most significant factor limiting the rate of progress. "Accumulation is the excess of production over consumption. If production is small, the sheer physical necessities of consumption press so hard upon the heels of the meager productive capacity that it requires the utmost parsimony and 'abstinence' to refrain enough from consuming to allow much accumulation. In such circumstances 'foreign investment,' i.e., an arrangement which enables the poor region to import without exporting, may be of great help in permitting the poor region to accumulate enough to start it on the path of progress."

Any discussion of Adam Smith is bound to be concerned with the degree to which practice today still follows theory. There are certain inevitable checks on the free operation of a free society. For one thing, the unchecked increase of population constantly presses upon technical progress.

But of more immediate concern is the intervention of the state in prosecuting wars of ever greater destructiveness. This must be deeply troubling to all Americans who realize the degree to which government spending for armaments helped at least through 1953 to sustain the postwar prosperity. Professor Boulding says it is doubtful that any of the wars of Adam Smith's century absorbed more than five per cent of national income. In contrast World War II absorbed up to fifty per cent of the national income of the major belligerents. It was a remarkable tribute to the rapidity of technical progress in the United States that this could happen while at the same time the standard of living rose rapidly out of the

remaining fifty per cent. But little optimism can be derived from this fact since the increase may be merely temporary with the outcome of the race between war and
peace still in doubt.

The philosopher, Professor Heimann, sees the immense
failures as well as the immense achievements of the system that owes so much to its early proponent. Capitalism
has failed to recognize frankly the power relationships
underlying the theory of automatic adjustment by self-
interest. "Productivity is bought at the expense of stability
since the former depends on more and more specialized
fixed capital and the latter on adaptabilty to ever more
rapidly changing conditions." Adam Smith had assumed
that the fluctuating market would gradually develop in
favor of labor. Market conditions did favor labor but not
steadily and the sweeping ups and downs of employment
brought home to the workers their degradation to mere
means for commercial ends. In Professor Heimann's view
that kept them all, employed and unemployed alike, in
uncertainty and fear which made a mockery of the concept of self-responsibility.

When we come to the lawyer, Professor Walton Hamilton formerly of the Yale Law School, his criticism is not
of Adam Smith and the eighteenth-century discovery that
self-interest was the spirit of the "progress" of mankind.
Adam Smith, unlike many of those who now quote him,
was too moral a man to venerate self-interest in the raw or
to endow a joint stock company with the civil rights of
persons. There are many critics, and Hamilton is among
them, who would trace present evils and abuses back to
the fact that the rights of the individual, as they evolved
out of our great inheritance from the past, have been con-
ferred on the corporation. In the interpretation of the
jurist, Adam Smith would pit the self-interest of one
against the self-interest of others and, if necessary, have

society interfere with its controls to make certain that the pursuit of gain was made to serve a public purpose.

It is vital to realize that Adam Smith did not seek to set up a system. His goal was to free the creative activities of mankind through the ever expanding production of goods exchanged with as little hindrance from government as possible. Nor did he give his unqualified blessings to the self-interest of the businessman as the prime mover of the greatest good in the best possible of worlds. Some of the latter-day disciples who are so fond of citing the prophet might be surprised at this warning from the master:

> "The proposal of any new law or regulation of commerce which comes from this order (business interest), ought always to be listened to with great precaution, and ought never to be adopted till after having been long and carefully examined, not only with the most scrupulous, but with the most suspicious attention. It comes from an order of men whose interest is never exactly the same with that of the public, who have generally an interest to deceive and even to oppress the public and who accordingly have upon many occasions both deceived and oppressed it."

The political economist, Professor John Maurice Clark of Columbia University, finds that as group power is less precisely limited by competitive checks, social responsibility in the use of that power becomes an absolute necessity. That is, it is a necessity if the industrial system is to go on working on a basis containing enough freedom to be fairly characterized as voluntary.

There were many limitations that Smith himself put upon the competitive process. He was deeply concerned over the deadening effect on workers' minds and characters of the monotonous jobs that the subdivision of labor was creating even in his time. Imagine Adam Smith viewing a Detroit assembly line or a high-speed steel mill in Pittsburgh! The author of "The Wealth of Nations" suggested education as a counter-measure to the deadening monotony of performing one single limited task day after day year in and year out. He approved of small religious sects because, among other benefits, they gave more people a chance to count for something in the life of a group.

In her comments in the volume, "American Income and Its Use," Professor Elizabeth Hoyt reminds us that Adam Smith sixteen years before publication of "The Wealth of Nations" had brought out his "Theory of Moral Sentiments." In that earlier work he expressed as well as it has ever been expressed the conviction that compassion and sympathy are fundamental emotions. They make man's concern for the well-being of his fellow man a strong motivating force touching every department of life. Adam Smith went so far in fact as to extend it to the whole world in a remarkable passage which Professor Hoyt quotes as follows:

"Though our effectual good offices can very seldom be extended to any wider society than that of our own country, our good will is circumscribed by no boundary, but may embrace the immensity of the universe. We cannot form the idea of any innocent and sensible being whose happiness we should not desire, or to whose misery, when distinctly brought home to the imagination, we should not have some degree of aversion. . . ."

Adam Smith is generally credited as being the founder of the laissez-faire school of economy, even though phrases with the same meaning were current long before he published his book. But he would be startled at the way the concept has been strained and stretched. Translated roughly laissez faire means permission to do as you will. It was the disciples following after the master who invented much of the dogma that today in popularized, vulgarized form passes under his name. It became part of the soaring optimism of the nineteenth century, that extraordinary epoch when, as had never happened before in recorded history, the population of the earth was doubled in a period of unprecedented peace and prosperity.

One of the most enthusiastic of the disciples was Claude Frédéric Bastiat, a popularizer whose "Economic Harmonies" was published posthumously in 1850. Economic laws, as understood by Bastiat, were translated into bright homilies that caught the popular fancy. For Bastiat "the acquisition of riches is of providential creation, natural, and consequently moral." This was ideally suited to the temper of the era which for all its surface smugness wanted to be assured that the great wealth derived from the mills spreading like a rash over the countryside was a part of God's purpose.

As Bastiat in France, so Henry Carey in this country spread the doctrine of complete laissez faire. This was reinforced in Carey's view by an unquenchable optimism over the boundless prospects for American prosperity. The outlook in the new continent with its still largely untouched resources was such as to refute the pessimistic conclusions of old-world philosophers. Carey ruled out the gloomy view of Malthus that an ever expanding population would constantly overtake technical progress and resources in such a way that hunger and misery would always catch up or run ahead of the human race. And Carey added another device to the laissez faire of Adam Smith. This was a protective tariff to safeguard developing industry. In America there need be no class conflict since labor's share of the total product would constantly increase and there would be a complete harmony of interest.

While men must associate with other men this would only strengthen individualism.

With some slight variations here and there this is the doctrine that still permeates much of the business community in America. A century after such apostles of optimism as Carey, the speeches at any service club luncheon could be taken almost literally out of the literature of a time when the transcendent virtues of individualism were first being proclaimed. In 1850 the new creed won ready response from eager and industrious individuals who were pushing back new frontiers not only in industry and finance but in every department of life. They wanted to be told that what they were doing was right and good, in the interests of both heaven and earth.

It seems to many today that the credo of individualism has worn a little thin; that its constant reiteration may arise from doubt as to its current validity. This is discussed by the contributors to "Goals of Economic Life." Thus Clark C. Bloom, Associate Professor of Economics at the University of Iowa, shows how even those who are most likely to preach "perfect competition" and the market mechanism rely on one form of government intervention or another. Professor Bloom concludes that we can no longer count on reaching economically correct results automatically, as a by-product of what individuals do in pursuit of their private interests. The element of practical ethics, he finds, has become an indispensable "factor of production."

Yet it is to the "dynamic" of the economics of Adam Smith that business men and many economists are more and more inclined to attribute the extraordinary gains in productivity of the American system. The Twentieth Century Fund underwrote a 777-page study, "Employment and Wages in the United States," by Professor W. S. Woytinsky and associates, published in 1953, which has this as its introductory note: "The economics of competition and the free market refute those who once argued that the American economy had reached a plateau." Professor Woytinsky finds that the rise of real wages in this country over the past century has carried the American living standard to top place in the world with an average increase of between one and two per cent a year. This has meant a real wage level today at least four times as great as that of a century ago. And there is no reason, in the view of the Woytinsky team, why average real earnings cannot rise over the next decade or two at an average of 2.5 to 3 per cent a year. "Euge! Belle! Dear Mr. Smith!"

Although many of today's most passionate preachers of individualism are hardly aware of it, a great deal of the religious and ethical framework out of the past has been carried over into the present. How important this heritage is to the order and stability in our own day the disciples of individualism sometimes almost willfully refuse to see. The conviction of a century ago was that pure self-interest and nothing else would make society run at the peak of greatest efficiency for the greatest good of all concerned. In "Social Responsibilities of the Businessman" Howard R. Bowen quotes the following from the *London Economist* of 1847:

> "It may be hurtful to the pride of statesmen to discover how little they can really do . . . to eradicate misery, to alleviate suffering, and improve society. Yet—so it is—the progress of civilization shows more and more how few and simple are the real duties of a government; and how impossible it is to add to those duties without inflicting permanent mischief on a community . . . But the aim of all statesmen who have acquired a higher reputation has been to remove regulations and restrictions imposed by others —to remedy the errors of former statesmen by removing old regulations, and not by *imposing new* ones.

All that can be said of the great statesman is that he discovered error and removed it; that he found a country harassed by restrictions and regulations, and that he freed it."

But even when the credo of individualism was being heralded as the ultimate triumph of the human mind, the conviction of laissez faire was not actually lived up to to the fullest extent. The successful functioning of the system clearly required reasonable adherence to a moral code. Beginning early in the nineteenth century there were restrictions put on the rights of the individual in the conduct of his own business. The early factory laws attempted to ameliorate somewhat the harsh lot of the working class. It was forbidden to employ children under six or seven for more than ten hours a day.

This has been consistently the direction with a complicated and voluminous body of law growing up to safeguard not only life and limb but liberty and the pursuit of happiness. Sometimes it has come only after a fierce struggle between opposing powers. But the process has been greatly helped by the example of moral men who felt themselves bound to do unto others as they would have others do unto them. It was greatly helped by the evangelical movement in the churches offering stern resistance to rampant individualism which would walk roughshod over the weak and the lowly. Without the frame of reference afforded by the religious and ethical inheritance of the past the laissez faire system might well have degenerated into chaos and violence. This is a profoundly important truth which those who today repeat the shibboleths of individualism too often do not understand or prefer to ignore.

CHAPTER III

The Contending Forces

THE BLIGHT SPREAD by the swiftly developing industrial revolution at the beginning of the nineteenth century is a commonplace of history. Both what was good and what was bad in the old order were rapidly vanishing from view. To a few this was an unmixed blessing, bringing prosperity of a kind never hitherto dreamed of. And that prosperity was underwritten by the laws of God and man.

But in its onset the revolution in production brought to most people confusion and misery. Dispossessed from the fields they had worked under the old system of land tenure, men, women and children migrated to the new industrial towns which were expanding in a crazyquilt pattern under a pall of soot. They worked ten, twelve, fourteen hours a day seven days a week in raw new factories where life and limb were the smallest consideration. To the degradation of Hogarth's Gin Lane out of the eighteenth century was added the spreading squalor of the jerry-built slum. One of the most searching and poignant pictures of what this meant is in Disraeli's novel "Sibyl or the Two Nations." It is a theme that gives a kind of ghastly incandescent illumination to much of Dickens' work. The misery, the shameless overcrowding, the incessant deadening toil, and the toll it took could not be exaggerated by artist or novelist.

The philosophy of individualism and self-interest had prepared the way for the acceptance of this "progress." One of the roots was Hume and his "An Inquiry Concerning the Principles of Morals." He had said that "the sole trouble Virtue demands is that of just Calculation and of steady preference of the greater Happiness." This was taken as a convenient prescription by many who wanted an intellectual foundation for the rights of property and for the liberty of the individual to do as he liked with himself and his own. This philosophy of individualism had gone a long way toward nullifying the authority of the monarch and the church. Both institutions, it might be added, had in the previous century contributed to the decay of their own authority by serious abuses of power and by their indifference to the welfare of the ordinary man.

To rationalism and individualism was joined one of the main currents of belief out of Rousseau—equality derived from the state of nature. As his contribution Archdeacon Paley supplied altruism which operated almost automatically "in obedience to the will of God and for the sake of everlasting happiness." All these streams of thought contributed to the concept of man as a beneficent egoist choosing, by reason of a kind of divine harmony plucked out of the air, the right rather than the wrong course. The conviction of a more or less fore-ordained goodness of the individual contributed much to the rise of democracy and utilitarian socialism. It was only a short step to the idea of the perfectibility of human society on earth through an all-powerful state capable of enforcing absolute justice.

The lyrical tributes to extreme individualism out of that time sound almost like hymns to anarchy. Thus the philosopher William Godwin writes, "The universal exercise of private judgment is a doctrine so unspeakably beautiful that the true politician will certainly feel infinite reluctance in admitting the idea of interfering with it." At first glance it may be difficult to see how the totalitarian state of Marxist communism could come out of this soil. But plainly if man was not naturally good, if he was not predestined to choose the way of virtue, and the first half of the nineteenth century afforded many striking examples that something was slightly wrong with this premise, then he would have to be made to be good. And since the authority of the church had largely been eliminated by the rationalist, individualist doctrine, the task of reforming man inevitably fell to the state, to which ever greater power had to be delegated. Merciless prophets of reform wanted to get on with the business by any means whatsoever even though it meant smashing the matrix of society in a holocaust of blood and fire and anguish. This is, of course, a great oversimplification but it may suggest why we find ourselves where we are today with the conflict between freedom and justice increasingly more acute.

Professor Knight in his discussion of this conflict points to the sobering fact that a society based on individual liberty and self-government is unique and recent. Furthermore, it has lost ground heavily in the past generation instead of rapidly conquering the world as was expected such a short time ago. On whether we can resolve conflicting claims—the right to accumulate and to pass on the accumulated fruits to one's heirs, the right to an equal or fair start in life, to a decent scale of living regardless of ability to make a sufficient productive contribution—may determine whether our kind of society is to survive. The early nineteenth century apostles of individualism would be dismayed to find Dr. Knight dismissing their literal individualism as untenable, absurd, and monstrous. Society is not in the main made up of responsible individuals at all, still less equally responsible. We are all the product of society and only in small part our own creation. And this gives pause to proposals to have society drastically remade by its members living at a particular date in history.

But the creed of individualism became in popularized form the everyday diet of every man. By the middle of the last century the doctrine of laissez faire had, in the words of John Maynard Keynes, been made milk for babes. It had, as he shows in his "Laissez-Faire and Communism," literally entered the nursery.

In 1850 the Society for Promoting Christian Knowledge was distributing wholesale a tract by Archbishop Whately with the title "Easy Lessons on Money Matters for the Use of Young People." The Archbishop admitted no doubts whatsoever about the individual and the supremacy of his rights. "More harm than good is likely to be done," the Archbishop concluded, "by almost any interference from government in men's money transactions, whether letting and leasing, or buying and selling of any kind." True liberty is "that every man should be left free to dispose of his own property, his own time and strength, and skill in whatever way he himself may think fit provided he does no wrong to his neighbor." The dogma had got hold of the educational machine. It had become a copybook maxim.

But while this was the going creed expressed in a thousand different ways at every level of acceptance, there were many who revolted against it. They saw all around them evidence contradicting the pat belief that the greatest good would result for the greatest number by each man's following to its inevitable end his own self-interest. The suffering and the degradation were too widespread to be ignored except by those who complacently wrapped themselves in one form or another of the prevailing dogma.

The rebellion took various forms. William Blake was

a flaming evangel with his angels of light ready to sweep down upon the iniquitous evils that were like a plague across the face of what had been green and peaceful England. In what has become in Britain a well-known hymn Blake expressed his sorrow and his anger:

> *And did the Countenance Divine*
> *Shine forth upon our clouded hills?*
> *And was Jerusalem builded here*
> *Among these dark Satanic mills?*

A later and more sophisticated interpretation suggests that perhaps the poet did not mean literally the mills that were belching forth smoke and maiming human lives but the philosophic mills at Oxford and Cambridge intended to justify the industrial revolution. But to many in the nineteenth century the mills of Satan were literally grinding the faces of the poor and lowly and mocking the human spirit. Angry critics sprang up. In 1850 Charles Kingsley published his pamphlet "Cheap Clothes and Nasty Clothes" which exposed the system of sweated labor. In a passage full of moral indignation he condemned the economic philosophy of his day:

> "I expect nothing from the advocates of laissez-faire—the pedants whose glory is in the shame of society, who arrogantly talk of economic science so completely perfected, so universal and all important that common humanity and morality, reason and religion must be pooh-poohed down, if they seem to interfere with its infallible conclusions, and yet revile, as absurd and utopian, the slightest attempt to apply those conclusions to any practical purpose. The man who tells us that we ought to investigate nature, simply to sit still patiently under her, and let her freeze, and ruin, and starve and stink us to death, is

a goose, whether he calls himself a chemist or a political economist."

John Ruskin turned from art to social criticism. He founded and endowed with a part of his fortune the Guild of St. George so as to promote village industries and model farming. Here was the yearning to find virtue and contentment in the handicrafts that had virtually disappeared as the machines of industry spewed out a growing stream of goods ever cheaper and more hideous. The same nostalgic backward look set William Morris and the pre-Raphaelites to painting and poetizing, making furniture and weaving tapestries in wistful imitation of a time forever gone.

For others revolted by the misery and horror in the proliferating industrial jungle the answer was not retreat. It was rather the reform of both man and society by the quickest short cut possible. This period marks the beginning of the long, still unresolved argument about human nature which one can hear in our time on almost any street corner. Education joined to a new social system, a kind of Christian socialism, that was the cure.

It was Robert Owen, one of the most interesting figures of this period, who may be said in a sense to have initiated the argument in its modern context. In any event he carried it on in terms that sound very familiar to us today. What we have come to know about human relations, the whole field of industrial psychology, is illuminated by the record left behind by this curious man and his remarkable and touching experiment.

Owen was a successful manufacturer who built a fortune by his own skill and industry in early nineteenth century England. But he soon became convinced that there were inherent wrongs in the system even though it had enabled him to advance himself so far and so fast. Setting out to right these wrongs, he first introduced reforms in his own factories which made them models for their day. But this was not enough for one who combined the reformer's zeal with an intensely practical drive.

To read Owen today is to get in pure form, unadulterated by a century of disillusioning experiment, the conviction that with a little trouble and pains the nature of man can be made over. He proposed the adoption of "nature's laws" to insure the "rationality of the human race." In a manifesto issued in Washington in 1844 he proclaimed that "the character of everyone, as soon as practicable, should be, from birth, recreated through a new creation and arrangement of superior external circumstances, and a new spirit thereby within it of charity, kindness and love." Through a correct knowledge of the eternal laws of humanity—Owen had no doubts on that score—he meant to replace without disorder or violence of any sort "all the inferior external circumstances of human creation with others, all useful, beneficial, and highly superior." This would eventually extend to "a federated union, without limit, over the Western Hemisphere."

Here in this social visionary with a practical bent were the germs of so much that was to come after, the plans, the federations, the hopes, the schemes, the societies for promoting this and that. In Owen's generous and uninhibited language was the attack on the stuff of human nature which was to be remolded into a pattern of triumphant virtue. We must, he said, "rebase, reorganize, reclassify, and reconstruct society." This was essential because "contrary to the inexperienced imaginations of our ancestors, individual man does not possess the power to create at his birth, the smallest part of his physical, mental or moral organization."

Determined to make over society, Owen decided to begin a large and generous experiment carrying out the principles in which he believed. Naturally the place for such an experiment was the New World. America was nearer, Owen thought, to a natural order of society, less involved in its own prejudices and dissensions, less under the domination of commercialism and class hostility. This conviction was colored in no small part by a belief in the goodness of the natural man living in a state of nature, a belief that stemmed from Rousseau. Owen was one of a stream of hopeful seekers who came to America expecting the very atmosphere to be endowed with this natural goodness.

There is something at once comic and pathetic about the innocent faith with which Owen undertook his experiment. On his arrival in America, he started off with a round of lectures to explain his grand project. The first of these lectures was delivered in the Hall of Representatives at Washington in the presence of the President and many of the leading public men of the day. He told his audiences why he had chosen America as a hopeful field for propaganda and experiment.

The scene of this heroic effort to reconstruct human society was New Harmony, Indiana, in Posey County on the banks of the Wabash River. The town had been founded in 1814 by a group known as the Harmonie Society but commonly called the Rappites because of the leadership of Father George Rapp who had been not only the founder, but prophet, priest, and king. These devout people believed in the early coming of the millennium. They thought to maintain what was then called Harmonie as a kind of annex to the Kingdom of Heaven on earth. Owen paid the Rappites £30,000 for the village and some 30,000 acres surrounding it. The town had been substantially built, the soil was good, and there was excellent pasture and orchard land. Besides cottages and public buildings the town included a silk and woolen mill. Here, seemingly, was the ideal location for the kind of utopia that Owen proposed to establish.

He invited "the industrious and well disposed of all

nations" to come to New Harmony. There was virtually no basis of selection for recruits to this latter day Eden in Indiana. Long before proper arrangements could be made for their reception or for putting them systematically to work 800 persons arrived. There was an acute need for skilled craftsmen and for building materials as a housing shortage developed. But despite these initial handicaps order was established. Schools were organized and concerts, recreations, and sports were set going.

Owen had intended that for the first three years New Harmony should remain under his personal control without any effort at self-government by the settlers. But so well did things seem to be going that he decided to appoint a committee to draw up a constitution. This was a time of eager enthusiasm. The communal constitution provided for the full equality of all settlers who were to function in six separate departments: agriculture; manufactures; literature, science, and education; domestic economy; general economy; and commerce. Each of the departments chose an "Intendant" who in turn chose four superintendents, these officers together forming the governing council of New Harmony. A man of great energy and practical ability, Owen in the initial phase used his managerial skills to keep the community at least on the surface contented and well regulated.

But differences and dissensions were not long in appearing. Dissatisfaction grew among the European disciples whom Owen had brought to Indiana. One of the most active dissenters refused to accept the constitution on the ground that it involved elections and representative government which were fatal to the free spirit of equality and community. The discord quickly spread. A split developed, and two groups of settlers formed on outlying parts of the estate separate communities of their own.

In Owen's original concept religion had not played an important part. While he himself held that a Supreme

Power was the cause of all existence, his own religion consisted in a rather generalized belief in charity and good will. The members of the community were at liberty to follow their own religious bent, which opened the way to further differences dividing the community into still smaller groups. From this point on the history of New Harmony is one of steady deterioration. One experiment in division and reunion followed another with a continuing relapse from the communal to an individual system and the individuals more and more disposed to war with each other.

In 1827 New Harmony was organized into a number of separate societies based on a kind of guild system. But every attempt at reconstruction quickly failed. Finally a good deal of the land was sold to individuals who were free to work it on their own. When the whole business was wound up Owen had lost about £40,000 which was four-fifths of his entire fortune.

This experiment has been related in detail because it is a classic example of the struggle of the earnest, well-intentioned idealist with the recalcitrant material of human nature. Owen's own conclusion is significant. He said it was premature to try to unite a number of strangers not previously educated for the purpose of living together in a common interest. Obviously a period of preliminary moral training was necessary before such an experiment could be successful.

This, too, has a familiar ring. In instance after instance later reformers who set out to tailor human society to some preconceived pattern of perfectibility have ended by confessing that the cloth was too tough, too thick, too thin, too weak. The little group of men who took power in Russia after the revolution of 1917 sought to cut the cloth of a whole people to fit an ideological pattern conceived in hatred and born of a moral arrogance blind to all considerations of mercy and humanity. The result has been unending cruelty and bloodshed in a despotism that has made the absolutism of the tsars look like a beneficent democracy.

It is a long way from the innocent, well meaning reformer on the banks of the Wabash to the men in the Kremlin who rule with an absolute power, self-destroying in its absoluteness. But in the intervening century we have come to understand more clearly the power relationships that are involved. We are beginning to realize what it means to put control in the hands of an ever-smaller number of managers. The interrelationship of power groups, some conscious and organized, others deriving from Adam Smith's conviction of self-interest at work in society, is explored by Kenneth Boulding in his study of "The Organizational Revolution." He finds that ethical restraints operate at many levels.

There are forces operating in society as there are within the human organism making for health. The doctor is the co-operator who can help redirect the forces making for health. The doctor of society—who is equally necessary— must also be a humble co-operator with the great forces of inter-action which often restore society to well-being in spite of his medication.

One of the chief self-restraining forces owes not a little to the evangelical movement stemming from John Wesley and the great revival of the eighteenth century. This is a part of the foundation, an important part of the heritage of the West, on which a free society has taken root and grown. The evangelical movement helped to provide a brake for the untrammeled self-interest of individuals pursuing the ends of their personal and private gain.

For John Wesley religion encompassed the whole of life. All economic problems were primarily ethical and therefore religious, since the true purpose of any creative economic theory and organization was the advancement of "human material well-being." "The earth is the Lord's and the fullness thereof," was the central theme of his economic faith. He believed in the divine proprietorship of all wealth, property, and privilege and, therefore, the responsible stewardship of the individual man. For Wesley any enduring antithesis between business and religion was unthinkable.

The great evangelist's famous money rule has often been quoted. It was: "Gain all you can. Save all you can. Give all you can." This injunction was circumscribed by the strictest limitations too often forgotten. Guided by "love toward God and man," the Christian must do "no harm" to his neighbor; he "must not sell anything which tends to impair health"; he must disassociate himself from all "hazardous and unhealthy employment." He must *gain* only by means which render true and honest service to his fellow men. Neither must he *save* to the extent of endangering the physical, mental, or moral health of his dependents or himself. One of Wesley's abiding fears was that by the virtues of industry and frugality man would lay up riches which would in turn produce pride and arrogance.

There were many who felt that even as he spoke the evidence was everywhere that these fears were more than justified. The rich had begun to accumulate wealth at an unprecedented rate. Great mercantile and industrial fortunes were being founded as the revolution in trade and manufacture swept everything before it in Britain, the workshop of the world.

But even the rich and powerful were touched by the evangelical revival. One of the notable converts was William Wilberforce who saw the evangelical light in 1785 after reading Dr. Doddridge's "The Rise and Progress of Religion." He had been up till that point a smart young dandy about London. A group gathered around Wilberforce that became known as "The Clapham Sect." They included some of the most influential men in London in the first half of the nineteenth century. Their common bond was evangelical Christianity and their common enthusiasm the application of the ethic of Christ to personal, social, political, national and international affairs. In Parliament their influence was out of all proportion to their numbers. Historians credit them with the beginning of a profound change in British colonial policy. They saw subject peoples in India and elsewhere in the Empire not as a vast mine to be exploited for the sake of British rulers but as a solemn, sacred trust to be developed for the highest good of the various peoples concerned.

Their great moral and idealistic fixation was on the abolition of slavery. Vast sums were raised through their efforts for the Anti-Slavery Society. The agitation led by Wilberforce and the Clapham Sect permeated the whole country. Wesley had condemned in his "Thoughts Upon Slavery" this "execrable sum of all the villainies." And he avowed that the grand idol of the whole traffic was "the god of gain." All its supporters and abettors he damned as "petty tyrants over human freedom." The tangible results coming in the first instance from the evangelical movement were extraordinary indeed. In a remarkably humane and disinterested act the British people through their Parliament paid twenty million pounds in advance to the West Indian planters to secure freedom for British slaves. England also paid £700,000 to Spain and Portugal to gain at least their wavering co-operation in suppressing the slave trade.

As the distinguished historian G. M. Trevelyan points out, evangelicalism brought rectitude, unselfishness, and humanity into high places and into the appeal to public opinion. But strangely enough the same humanitarians who gave so much to free the Negroes from slavery were more often than not callous and indifferent to the sufferings of the English poor under the transformation wrought by the industrial revolution. In this respect they differed but little from the employers and landlords who were known by the significantly descriptive phrase "the high and dry." Hannah More, another convert from London society, and her friends, sincerely believed that inequalities of fortune did not really matter since they would be redressed in the next world. These good people distributed tracts among laborers who could make scarcely enough to live on by working 80, 90, and 100 hours a week, tracts seeking to persuade them that it was to their spiritual advantage to be abjectly poor provided that they were submissive to their superiors. Wilberforce helped persuade the willing Pitt that it was his duty to pass the combination laws rendering trade unionism illegal.

But the force of the evangelical movement, with its continuing insistence carried out of the past on the relevancy of religion to man's daily life, came to have a wider influence bearing directly on the status of ordinary men and women everywhere in the West. It is hardly an exaggeration to say that the devoutly religious reformers who came out of the evangelical revival were responsible for freeing the industrial slaves in England. The leader of the movement was Lord Shaftesbury who in his 60 years of public life did perhaps more than any single individual, through a whole series of laws put on the statute books, to improve the status of workers. He led the way for the enactment of what was called the Ten Hours Act and the Mines and Collieries Act, sometimes called the Magna Carta of industrial liberty. Preliminary steps in this direction were the Factory Acts of 1833, 1844, and 1850, while the industrial extension acts of 1864 and 1867 made the reforms applicable to virtually all of labor throughout the British Isles.

Associated with Shaftesbury, who was the first president of the Young Men's Christian Association, were others equally devout and dedicated who had been caught up in the fervor of the evangelical revival. John Wood, the great cotton mill owner, largely financed the Ten Hours Crusade. Richard Oastler, who was known as "the Factory Children's King," was the son of a preacher who was disinherited by his father for his Methodism. J. R. Stephens, an ordained Methodist minister, served 18 months in prison because of the unparliamentary nature of his popular agitation for factory reforms. Michael Sadler, who instigated the famous Sadler's Report on Factory Conditions in 1831 exposing the shameful exploitation of women and children as well as men, was the superintendent of a large Sunday school in Leeds.

All this was happening, it must be borne in mind, while the philosophy of self-interest as the key to a happy society was being expounded in its purest and most unadulterated form. Out of a deep religious conviction these ardent Victorians were preaching to all who would listen that it was immoral to keep ten or twelve or more people living in one room in a foul-smelling slum; to make them work from dawn to dark in an ill-lighted, ill-ventilated jerry-built factory for scarcely subsistence wages. This is a striking instance of the relevancy of religion to business at the very time when business was supposed to have emancipated itself from all restraints.

A continuing reform movement, including the Chartist agitation of 1838 to 1848, expressed the widespread discontent amounting almost to revolt of the British people against the grim condition of their lives. In established Chartist churches the spirit and teaching of early Christianity attracted numbers of men and women who found both the Anglican Church and the Methodist Chapel cold and unsympathetic. "The political economists in Church and State," said The *Crisis,* a Chartist paper, commenting on the new slum towns, "are the real high priests of the realm. They have set up the golden calf . . . impious, dissatisfied people, say they, you men without property, scum of the earth, with minds born to inferiority and hands made for our service. Why if you are still discontented do you not seek to accumulate wealth and so become respectable like ourselves?"

The Chartist movement was but one phase of the reform movement. There was the National Association for the Protection of Labor which soon gained 100,000 members. In 1833 Robert Owen established the Grand National Consolidated Trade Union which took in agricultural laborers and women workers, many later Chartists, for whom organization and self-protection seemed impossible except under the spur of despair or religious devotion or both. Although the Chartist movement went down in defeat, it was a moral and ethical force that left a strong imprint on the time. Lord John Russell admitted that the Chartist movement had turned the mind of the ruling class toward problems of health, education, and trade unionism with its demand for at least minimum standards of safety, decency, and wages.

While the Oxford movement was in its origin scholastic and religious, with the aim of restoring the authority of the church and the place of the sacraments, it contributed to a more immediate concern for the problems of ordinary people caught in the cross-currents of revolutionary change. The Anglo-Catholic movement, coming a little later, was also concerned in part at least with relating religion to the problems of daily life. The clergy in the Anglican Church had been for at least 100 years scarcely more than a learned branch of the squirearchy, hunting and shooting and vying with each other for rich "livings." Now the effort was to get the parson out of the hunting field and to make him see that the exploitation of the colonies and the exploitation of women and children in the industrial slums were not walled off in a remote department of life which was none of his business.

In our time we have grown sophisticated and perhaps even cynical about movements of reform. But it is important to remember that out of the light kindled by Wesley and the evangelical revival came the great drive for reform movements that has had a direct and continuing relationship to the life of the past 100 years. It is hard to imagine how society could have adhered and endured without the ameliorating influence of this force. The YMCA, the temperance movement, the societies for the prevention of cruelty to children and animals, the Salvation Army, these and many other such currents flowed out of the faith that held that religion was for daily life as well as for the closet and the cloister.

In America these same movements of reform took root and were profoundly influential in shaping the course of American life. While the motivations were different, related more nearly to the needs of a people pioneering in a land often harsh and hostile, the origins were much the same. The evangelical fervor sometimes veered in a fundamentalist direction, with the emotionalism of the camp meeting as an outlet. But it was related to temperance, to better schools, and in rural America to a sense of fair play as between the farmer and the capitalist on the Eastern seaboard who controlled the railways and thereby dominated the freight rates.

In this way the farmer was robbed of the fruits of his toil. Or so hundreds of thousands of men and women on the farms of the West came to believe as they joined in a variety of organized protest movements. The Populists and similar organizations of revolt which took hold as the West filled up were based on a people dedicated to a religion that exacted much in this world. Godliness, plain living, hard work, thrift, these were the virtues that would bring prosperity and contentment, an increase of family and lands, a tranquil old age and finally a just reward in Heaven. And if these virtues went unrewarded, then something was wrong—the monopoly of the railroads and the squeeze put on the farmer by the railroad promoter.

Behind the protest movements that again and again set the prairies afire was the awareness, whether expressed or implied, of a direct and continuing relationship between religion, the ethics of daily living, and the rewards and penalties not only of the life hereafter but on earth as well.

This was the background as the era of the rise of the great corporations—the organizational revolution—was beginning. Thus was added another layer of what Professor Boulding has called the "common morality" of our Western culture, built up by long testing and accretion in societies where organizations had been for the most part small, and ethics was on a person-to-person basis.

CHAPTER IV

Modern Man and Modern Dogma

AT THIS MIDPOINT of the twentieth century there are
deeply held and widely shared fears that man has surren-
dered his destiny to forces beyond his control. Events have
succeeded each other with such terrible swiftness, seeming
to override the individual conscience and the conscience
of society as well, that no choice may be left but to yield to
impersonal forces of an order dwarfing the ethical considerations out of the past. To many, these forces appear
to be overwhelming, completely deterministic, in a sense
predestined to prevail.

While it cannot be said to be the universal or even the
dominant mood, nevertheless it is not surprising that a
pessimism, a gloomy kind of fatalism, should color the
outlook of many thoughtful people. A reason, and
perhaps in itself a sufficient reason, is the phenomenon of
mass warfare unique to the twentieth century. The best of
a whole generation walked out to death at Passchendaele,
the Somme, the Argonne in the first world war. War had
been confined before largely to the professional soldiery
and only in rare instances in history, when catastrophe was
piled upon catastrophe as in the Thirty Years' War, had
entire peoples been subjected to prolonged suffering, fam-
ine, and death. In the second world war the mass annihila-

tion rained on the cities, first through conventional ex-
plosives dropped by great armadas of bombers on cities
such as London, Rotterdam, Berlin, and Hamburg, and
finally at the end the atomic bombing of Hiroshima and
Nagasaki carried the process forward close to total
destruction.

But awesome and overwhelming as these events have
been, they do not entirely explain the sense of foreboding,
the sense of powers outside the human scale, that permeates not a little of the thinking in the West. This may
be in part a consequence of one of the elements that as
much as any single influence helped to create the climate
of our time. That is the determinism stimulated by
Darwin and developed as a major theme by the leading
thinkers of the later nineteenth century. The current of
determinism that appeared to be confirmed and then re-
confirmed by the scientific "progress" of the time swept
a great deal before it, including one cannot say precisely
how much of the ethical responsibility of the individual.

The individual could scarcely be expected to resolve
the struggle between his conscience and his desires since
he was told that he was merely a small part of a process
that was advancing with an inevitability predetermined
beyond his control and in a large measure beyond his
comprehension. The history of the last century has at
times the look of a morality play, with the individual conscience buttressed by the ethical and religious inheritance
from the past contending with the dogma of inevitability;
the inevitability of progress on the one hand, the inevitability of doom on the other hand.

In the Middle Ages the center of the concern of the
Church was for extension of its sway and the salvation of
the soul of the individual. The relationship was that between God and man with God's ministers on earth inter-
mediaries and interpreters between the one and the other.
Despite the concept of predestination, Calvinism and the

Puritan Reformation that came out of it tended to transfer much of the burden for personal salvation to the individual man. The individual was required to work in partnership with God, under the close supervision of the religious community, to achieve his own salvation. And as a part of that salvation he was required to advance the Kingdom of Heaven on earth by his industry and his virtue.

But in the dogma deriving from Darwin, or more accurately from the innumerable popularizers and vulgarizers of Darwinism, neither God nor man had very much to do with the human animal and the nature of the society he had organized. This was the revolutionary contribution of the main stream of thought of the nineteenth century and its far-reaching consequences have been but dimly perceived. The catchwords, phrases such as "the survival of the fittest," came to take hold far down in the consciousness of the mass mind of the West. These catch phrases seemed to justify a surrender of the individual to forces beyond his control. He was part of a biological process that had brought him to his present position of superiority in the world and these same forces still at work, in large measure beneficently, relieved him of the necessity for any narrow choice as between good and evil. He had survived, he was therefore the fittest. In the mirror he saw the flattering image of the superman, a god-like destiny.

It was but a short step from the evolution of the species to the evolution of the society he had shaped. The dogma out of Darwinism came to have its special force when the theory of evolution was translated from the sphere of biology to sociology. In the popular notion, it was not merely that man was transcendent but the social order that he evolved from the slime was likewise a product of evolution, having gone from bad to good to better. And at the top of the happy escalator on which he had so for tuitously been placed was inevitably the best. If you had come this far from a monkey, how could you end up as anything but a kind of god? That easy assumption came to be more and more taken for granted as the idea of a ceaseless and almost effortless progress caused even the clouds in the brilliant nineteenth century sky to glow with a radiant promise.

It was Herbert Spencer who did more than anyone else to translate the biological values of the evolution of the species into social values of his own definition. This egocentric philosopher, who had a more or less self-made mind, exerted a widespread influence that is hard for us to understand today when we look back at the ponderous, doctrinaire volumes that one after another to the age of nearly 80 he gave to a waiting world. The explanation may lie in the fact that his philosophy of triumphant self-interest happened to coincide with the needs and the desires of the leaders in business and public life in the century of unbroken optimism and prosperity.

The principles of biology, the principles of psychology, the principles of sociology, the principles of ethics, these Spencerian achievements loomed large against the intellectual horizon of their time. They all underwrote in one degree or another the position of extreme individualism that Spencer maintained throughout his life.

His basis of judgment, both for the individual and for the society of which he was a part, was the law of the struggle for existence. In maintaining his position he was often led into an authoritarian arbitrariness in support of the laissez faire that he saw as the root of all virtue. He came up with a code of "absolute ethics." This would be achieved in a state of social harmony so complete that the lion of egoism would gladly lie down with the lamb of altruism and there would forever be peace between them. Everyone would derive egoistic pleasure from doing altruistic acts that would still be needed in this ideal state of

affairs. God for Spencer was the Unknowable. Since
Spencer's unknowable was also inscrutable, there was
something of a contradiction inasmuch as it seemed to
reduce all knowledge to a dubious, not to say precarious,
status.

Both in Britain and in America his influence was widespread. Translated into popular terms, his philosophy
provided a sort of certificate of good behavior for the
rising group of industrialists. It seemed to bless, too, the
far-flung expansion of the colonial powers. The Spencerian dogma was a corollary to the bland confidence of the
foreign missionary that he was carrying a superior religion to peoples with inferior religions.

The civilization of the white man, his pattern of industry and trade, was so obviously better than anything else
ever conceived by the mind of man or the hand of God
that it was the duty of the native to accept it just as he
must accept Christianity. The conquest of Africa, with
all its cruelties and horrors, the disruption of an ancient
way of life that had its own virtues in inner stability, was
blessed by the convenient assumptions of the day that
owed not a little to the popular conviction of the "survival of the fittest."

From the perspective of our time one marvels at the
confidence of the titans of that other age. Spencer came
into conflict in 1893 with the great biologist, Thomas
Huxley. In a lecture at Oxford Huxley had challenged
Spencer's evolutionary ethics. "The practice of that which
is ethically best—what we call goodness or virtue—" Huxley had said, "involves a course of conduct which, in all
respects, is opposed to that which leads to success in the
cosmic struggle for existence. In place of ruthless self-
assertion it demands self-restraint." Spencer wrote a long
essay to prove that the ethical process and, by implication,
the ethical man, are products of the cosmic process for, he
asked, with a fresh sort of innocence, if the ethical man

is not a product of the cosmic process, what is he a product
of? Finally after a somewhat circuitous explanatory route
the philosopher declared that he and the biologist were
in fact in agreement. In a reply to Huxley, Spencer concludes the argument with this statement:

"... We agree in denouncing the brutal form of
the struggle for existence. We agree that the struggle
for life needs to be qualified when the gregarious state
is entered, and that among gregarious creatures lower
than man a rudiment of the ethical check is visible.
We agree that among men the ethical check, becoming more and more preemptory, has to be enforced
by the society in its corporate capacity, the state. We
agree that beyond that qualification of the struggle
for life which consists in restricting the activities of
each so that he may not trench upon the spheres for
the like activities of others, which we call justice,
there needs that further qualification which we call
beneficence; and we differ only respecting the agency
by which the beneficence should be exercised. We
agree in emphasizing, as a duty, the effort to mitigate
the evils which the struggle for existence in the social
state entails . . ."

Significant in this passage is the admission that the
ethical check must be enforced by the state. Here, it must
seem to us today, was one of the chief flaws in the structure erected by the prophets of the nineteenth century's
onward and upward theory of progress. At first glance
it seems a small flaw. But if beneficence does not in fact
evolve according to schedule, if the treacherous and stub-
born stuff of human nature does not behave in accord
with theory, then in a complex society an ever greater
and greater recourse must be had to the state, that is to
say the policeman. As we have seen in the years since

Spencer, the role of the state is not just that of the policeman. In a more and more complex economy tending to monopoly concentration, the state must function as stabilizer, helping to establish a balance of forces. But the degree of intervention by the state, whether as policeman, stabilizer, or whatever, remains a highly controversial question.

Yet this flaw was seemingly not visible at the time. The prospect was so beguiling—man the transcendent being moving steadily upward on the biological-philosophical escalator toward a not too distant landscape rosy with the promise of final perfection. And all around was the confirmatory evidence in invention, discovery, ever-increasing productivity, the civilization of the white man carried across the farthest desert and ocean. There were few to look for flaws. Only now and then doubters like Ruskin asked awkward questions. When a journalist came to him for comment on the opening of the cable to India, he replied by asking, "But what do you have to say to India?"

This is not to say that the dogma out of Darwin by way of Spencer was accepted unquestioningly and unhesitatingly. On the contrary, in America in particular it provoked a long and heated controversy that continued down almost to our own day. It would, however, be accurate to say that it became increasingly the fashionable and prevailing doctrine. It was embraced by "advanced thinkers" prepared to believe that civilization was soon to reach a glorious apogee, a happy peak on which presumably it would remain poised for all eternity.

Many ministers of the Gospel denounced the theory of evolution and all its works. Many saw in it an ominous challenge to the truth as revealed in the Bible. Others found it Godless, materialistic, full of man's arrogance and pride. But the proof that social evolution, underwriting the concept of inevitable progress, had become high fashion was seen in its embrace by one of America's popular divines of the latter half of the nineteenth century. The noted preacher, Henry Ward Beecher, had a reputation greater than that of a movie star or a baseball pitcher in our day. In 1882 in a highly publicized sermon the Reverend Mr. Beecher publicly declared his belief in the idea of evolution as transmuted through Spencer. He said that after studying the doctrine for twenty years he had come to the conclusion that it was irresistible. One senses in this a bandwagon movement. Christianity, and even the Reverend Mr. Beecher himself, could evolve into ever more beautiful and perfect forms.

For a society that had so deliberately immersed itself in a warm bath of optimism, working industriously and perseveringly to keep the temperature up, the perfect form of expression was the World's Fair. Beginning with the exposition of 1850 at London in the famous Crystal Palace, one after the other they celebrated progress and the triumph of man employing nature's laws. The Chicago World's Fair of 1893 was one of those occasions when men and women interrupted their industriousness to congratulate each other on their achievements.

There was not a single cloud in the sky. This was the culmination of the ages sprung up from the swamps that had once surrounded Ft. Dearborn. It was characteristic of the time that there should be held in connection with the Fair a Parliament of Religions and a Congress of Evolutionists. Large audiences attended both the Parliament and the Congress and the one following the other they seemed related to the same business of keeping mankind on the track of the better heaven and the better earth. The evolutionists heard some stirring papers—"The Beastliness of Modern Civilization—Evolution the Only Remedy," "The Constructive Power of Evolution," "The Influence of the Doctrine of Evolution on Ethical Standards."

But the main feature was a paper written for the Congress by Herbert Spencer and read to the delegates. As reported in the press, the great man told them that if society were to continue to develop for the production of the greatest general happiness altruistic activities were essential as well as egoistic activities and that a due share of them was obligatory upon each citizen. In other words the process was not completely automatic. Yet reading that essay called "Social Evolution and Social Duty" one finds in it, despite the insistence on the necessity for conscious altruism as well as egoism, the expression in its purest form of the philosophy that transfused the popular thinking of the day.

The critics had said that once evolution was erected into the paramount law of man's moral and social life it would produce a paralyzing and amoral fatalism. In his address to the delegates to the Congress of Evolutionists in Chicago, Spencer set out to answer this charge by neatly balancing off altruism and egoism. One finds him, however, in the following remarkable passage coming back to the belief that was central to his philosophy and to so much of the thought of the day:

"... It is true that much social evolution is achieved without any intention on the part of citizens to achieve it, and even without the consciousness that they are achieving it. The entire industrial organization in all its marvelous complexity has risen from the pursuit by each person of his own interest, subject to certain restrictions imposed by the incorporated society; and by this same spontaneous action have arisen also the multitudinous appliances of industry, science and art, from flint knives up to automatic printing machines, from sledges up to locomotives—a fact which might teach politicians that there are at work far more potent social agencies than those which they control."

In the history of the past hundred years we are beginning to realize how deeply the current of determinism, one might almost say automatism, influenced the development of both of the forms of organization, capitalism and communism, coming out of this period. In its origin communism was bound to an orthodoxy so narrow, so dogmatic, that it is difficult to see how it could have developed in any fashion other than it has. This would appear to be true even if the experiment of communism had not first been undertaken on a large scale in Russia, where centuries of tyranny and a kind of Chinese wall keeping out the West had prepared a passive people to accept a new and far more thoroughgoing kind of despotism.

In a time in which personal choice and personal responsibility—the conscience of the individual—have been blurred and confused by the rise of great impersonal forces, one of the attractions of communism is that it promises the surrender of the will. The will and the conscience are reposed in a depository of granite solidity under a guardianship that resolves all ethical and moral problems. This necessity of individual surrender permeates Marxism from beginning to end. It is fundamental to the outlook of the founder of communism. In another age Marx might have been a religious prophet of the blood and brimstone variety. He had a deep and real conviction of the evils of industrialism. This conviction took the form, within the frame of the determinist and authoritarian philosophy of Hegel, of what amounted to a religious system; a religious system devoid of a beneficent god and of any vestige of mercy. But the moral categories were as absolute as any the world has ever seen.

In the view of this avenging prophet everything bourgeois was bad, wicked, corrupt. It was inevitably doomed by its own corruption, its own contradiction, its own inherent evil. In other words the escalator was moving downward, carrying the owners, the bosses, their paid hirelings of the press, and other bourgeois dependencies. Reaching the bottom, with the inevitable breakdown of the bourgeois economy, they would be destroyed in a Wagnerian apocalypse of fire and blood. After this denouement the "good" workers would take over and begin the building of the perfect socialist state. From this point on there were way stations along the route, including the period necessary for the withering away of the state, but the progress was to be nearly automatic and self-regulating.

There is an increasing recognition of the attraction that communism exerts as a kind of religion; a false religion but one nevertheless with the same moral imperatives of heaven and hell, good and evil. As Professor Boulding points out, in the "materialist" outlook of Marxism the idealogy, religion, and institutions of man are not independently determined but are mere creatures of the techniques of production. Nevertheless from the viewpoint of Marxism as an ethical system, the dialectical materialist interpretation of history plays much the same role as the concept of the will of God in Christian ethics. It is, says Professor Boulding, an omnipotent force which requires the individual to give his voluntary consent. Therefore in Marxism as in Calvinism the individual is called upon to exert his efforts toward salvation. In Boulding's view those Marxists have been heretics who have maintained that because the dialectical process was invincible and inevitable there was no necessity to enlist in the class war—one could simply wait for the glorious revolution to come about. The orthodox are those who invoke the rallying cry, "Workers of the World, Unite!" even though at first glance this seems incompatible with the automatic processes of history laid down in the gospel of Marx.

The moral categories are, however, as rigidly set forth as in any primitive religion. They are as final, as arbitrary, as inviolable. Dr. Charles Lowry in his scholarly study "Communism and Christ" has analyzed the appeal of Marxism as a fake religion. As Professor Boulding says, this may be one of the most important reasons for the attraction Marxism has exercised during the past century. It is just here that the most searching examination of the Western outlook, an honest self-examination of the Western mind, becomes essential. The surrender of intelligent young Westerners brought up with every educational advantage to the Marxist doctrine to such a degree that they became tools of the Communist conspiracy is a most profoundly troubling phenomenon no matter how limited it may be. It is perhaps better understood in the context of a search for an absolute, a great and seemingly unquestionable body of authority in which the uneasy burden of the will and the conscience may be laid down. The reasons why the desire to surrender should be strong are many and diverse.

It is enough to suggest here that the influence of the determinist viewpoint out of the nineteenth century may have played a part greater than has been suspected. We must ask the question whether or not it prepared the way also for the surrender of the will; for the alienation that must have occurred before an intelligent young Westerner could embrace the dogma of Marx as exemplified in the police state that is the Soviet Union.

This question of the divorcement of the individual from the roots of Western society deserves far more consideration than it has been given. In his little book called "Laissez-Faire and Communism" John Maynard Keynes has some trenchant things to say about Communism as a set of religious beliefs. Keynes visited Russia in 1925 and reported that he had found it, as a man of intellect, thoroughly repellent. Sympathizing with those

seeking something good in Soviet Russia, he went on,
and this was nearly thirty years ago, to add:

"But when we come to the actual thing, what is
one to say? For me, brought up in a free air undark-
ened by the horrors of religion, with nothing to be
afraid of, Red Russia holds too much which is de-
testable. Comfort and habits let us be ready to
forgo, but I am not ready for a creed which does not
care how much it destroys the liberty and security
of daily life, which uses deliberately the weapons
of persecution, destruction, and international strife.
How can I admire a policy which finds a characteristic expression in spending millions to suborn spies
in every family and group at home, and to stir up
trouble abroad? Perhaps this is no worse and has
more purpose than the greedy, warlike, and imperial-
istic propensities of other Governments; but it must
be far better than these to shift me out of my rut.
How can I accept a doctrine which sets up as its
bible, above and beyond criticism, an obsolete economic textbook which I know to be not only scien-
tifically erroneous but without interest or application for the modern world? How can I adopt a creed
which, preferring the mud to the fish, exalts the
boorish proletariat above the bourgeois and the in-
telligentsia who, with whatever faults, are the quality
in life and surely carry the seeds of all human advancement? Even if we need a religion, how can we
find it in the turbid rubbish of the red bookshops?
It is hard for an educated, decent, intelligent son of
Western Europe to find his ideals here, unless he has
first suffered some strange and horrid process of conversion which has changed all his values."

It is this conversion which should concern us. Is it

not possible that while Keynes, the agnostic, failed to comprehend it, the conversion is in large part a consequence of the alienation of intelligent young Westerners from the ethical values that have come out of the religious inheritance of the past? The further step to Communism was a relatively small one once the alienation, the conversion, had already taken place. Many intelligent young Westerners have had an occasion to regret bitterly their lapse into Communism. It should be added that many Westerners with a deeply idealistic bent saw a terrible contradiction between the ethical values professed by the West and Western civilization. They were able to believe that Communism had resolved the contradictions that seemed so glaring in the West. Pacifists took at face value the peace-loving professions of Moscow and the denunciation of "imperialist warmongers." It may thus be an oversimplification to ascribe the defection to a process of alienation. Yet if Lord Keynes' intelligent young Westerner had not been divorced from the mainsprings of Western culture and Western morality, he surely would not have so easily swallowed the Communist professions.

But if we are candid we must ask ourselves whether those who rejected freedom did so, in part at least, because the appeal of free enterprise, the free choice, had lost its meaning? Was it because the philosophy, the doctrine, of a free society had become so materialistic that it no longer evoked a response to the impulse toward idealism and belief that is inherent in almost everyone?

Such questions cannot be answered with finality. But certain observations may be ventured. First it is true that the free enterprise system, that is to say capitalism in its extraordinary development over the past century, has never had anything like the frame of dogma which enclosed the Communist system. That is at one and the same time an advantage and a disadvantage.

It is one of the reasons why a pluralistic as opposed to a monolithic society has been possible. Many voices have been heard. Many choices are evident even on the lower levels of society. This is the theme that runs through Howard Bowen's "Social Responsibilities of the Businessman." Although there has been an increasing tendency to divorce ethics and religion from the concerns of business, in accord with the dogmatic assertion that no restraints whatsoever must be imposed upon the process of expanding productivity, the ethical-religious voice has continued to exert a profound influence in every sphere of life.

The laissez faire dogma held, in a mordant metaphor, that under the gospel of Darwin crossed with Adam Smith the strong, tall giraffes in the social corral would be able to crop all the tender succulent nourishing leaves. They would thus inevitably triumph over the short, feeble giraffes who would be trampled out of the way so that starvation and death would overtake them. But religious and humanitarian impulses, the two often inextricably intertwined, were constantly interfering with the working of this thesis. Ardent and dedicated reformers, in America women in particular such as Florence Kelley and Jane Addams, worked tirelessly against the abuses of the factory system and the inhuman overcrowding of helpless immigrants in the slums of the great cities. No one can doubt that they greatly affected both attitude and custom. They prepared the way for the system of social security that was to follow. Similarly the rise of the trade unions as a separate force prepared the way for the eight-hour day and the five-day week and vacations with pay.

But the dogmatic aspects of the free-enterprise ideology produced strains and tensions evident in our society today. Certain deeply held beliefs persist long after circumstances have made them invalid. In the study "American Income and Its Uses," which we will consider later at greater length, some of the strains on the modern family are analyzed.

The belief has been deeply held, coming in part out of our pioneering past, that a family looks after its own members who may be sick or old or destitute. But the family has undergone a swift transformation in recent decades, above all in response to the demand from industry for unfailing mobility. The wage earner must be prepared to move on little or no notice from one region to another or from one industry to another. The family today often lives in a small apartment in a great city with no room for the aged and no outlet for the energies of growing children.

It has not been easy to accept a system of social security under which many of the family responsibilities of the past are assumed by the state. This goes against some of the most deeply ingrained impulses associated with a family dwelling place to which under adverse circumstances all might have recourse for food and shelter. There were deep and abiding satisfactions in that system with its roots in a way of life coming down from the Biblical era.

In fact the wisdom, the profound pervasive truths of the Bible, come out of the experience of the clan family. But that kind of family could not survive in a highly developed commercial-industrial society. Where it has persisted it may well have been a factor in retarding industrialization. China with the persistence of the patriarchal family, extending the umbrella of its protection over innumerable relatives down to the remotest connection, was an interesting instance of this retardation.

The clan family, working and sharing, all for one and one for all in its idealization, tended to minimize the responsibility of the individual. It is in the injunction

put on the individual to succeed, to make good, to contribute or to be cast aside that the dogma of free enterprise bears down hardest. This injunction is constantly
reiterated in every fashion by every medium from child-
hood onward. The intense competitiveness it inspires is
one reason ours is such a dynamic society.

But this competitiveness means for many a great and
continuing strain. The injunction to compete is enforced on all including those who must start at a disadvantage with a sense of injustice and inequality. In their
study of contemporary problems of family support, carried out in the project on Ethics and Economic Life, J. L.
McConnell and Janet M. Hooks show how under conditions of modern industrialism the children both of broken
families and of large families are penalized. The increase in family instability and breakdown, of which the
sensational increase in the divorce rate is a consequence,
leaves many children in the care of one parent, more
commonly the mother, who may be unable to meet the
family's financial needs. According to census estimates
made in 1949, the median income of one-parent families
was $1,597 while the median income for families with both
parents was $3,174.

As these same authors observe, some families have con-
siderably more of the good things of life than others
and are therefore able to give their children a much more
favorable start. Preliminary data from the 1950 census
shows that one-fifth of the families and unrelated individuals with the highest incomes received 47 per cent
of the total income of the country. On the other hand
the poorest one-fifth received only three per cent of the
total national income. The same figures showed that
one-fourth of all families had incomes below $2,000 and
one-fourth of all children were in these families. Three-
fifths of the children in families at these low levels were
one of three or more children. Even at income ranges

above the lowest, the authors observe, it is clear that an
income adequate for a family without children may
represent a poverty level when there are several children.
Too often these differences are ignored. Those who
have had the advantages blandly assume that the race
in which they are ahead has been an equal one. While
we have outgrown the innocence of Horatio Alger, we
believe that it is still possible to overcome the severest
handicaps both social and economic. And each of us can
cite many examples to prove that this is still a reality.
Nothing like the caste identification of birth, accent, man-
nerisms which still persists in Great Britain has ever been
established in this country except in a few isolated en-
claves on the Eastern Seaboard and in the South.

Yet the burden of competitiveness on the disadvan-
taged, the fear of failure, the threat of insecurity can become intolerable. Particularly is this true when the handi-
cap is due merely to the accident of birth as in the dis-
crimination against race, color, and creed. Dr. Stanley A.
Leavy and Dr. Lawrence Z. Freedman of the Department of Psychiatry of the Yale School of Medicine have
studied the connection between psychoneurosis and economic life and reported it in the fifth volume of the Ethics
and Economic Life project.

A series of case studies indicates the direct relationship between the strains imposed in a competitive society
and emotional illness. The two doctors cite a survey made
in 1940 in Baltimore showing that the incidence of neurosis was twice as great for persons on relief as for those
who had an income of two thousand dollars and over.
A study now going forward at Yale reveals a striking
correlation between social level and the incidence of
schizophrenia, which is perhaps the commonest form of
emotional disturbance. Some nine times as many patients
in the lowest or "class five" level suffer from schizo-

phrenia as would be expected if this illness occurred equally distributed throughout the social organization. According to the two psychiatrists, patients commonly report as one of their deepest sources of neurotic guilt that they have not been able to provide more fully for their families.

As a measure of success, money, with the things it buys, has become paramount; so much so that workers today are not aware at first hand of being deprived of the satisfaction that was once present in the making of a finished object. In contrast economic failure and hardship set up a threat within as well as without. One is shamed before one's fellows, and this sense of shame undermines the confident personality. "It is the sensitive relationship between social values exacting economic success and the self-esteem of the individual which makes competition likely to contribute to the development of neurosis."

While the values of one period may be totally irrelevant to another, they persist as part of the individual's outlook on the world. With the depression that began in 1929 millions were unable to find employment in every country of the West. Most of the world was in the grip of great impersonal forces that had come to a shattering climax. Yet in the face of this terrible reality, many who were more fortunate and who had carried over from another time a belief in the saving grace of industry and thrift remained convinced that the jobless were lazy or negligent. In her moving study of this phenomenon, "Some Folks Won't Work," published as the depression was beginning, Clinch Calkins showed how the persistence of this attitude contributed to an atmosphere of mutual hostility and distrust in which rational discussion of what to do about the millions of unemployed was made more difficult. There was something shameful about it all, and we wanted to keep it out of sight as long as possible.

Profound changes in the attitudes of most people have taken place since then. Far from proposing to abolish the basic reforms of the New Deal era, a Republican administration came to power in 1953 with promises to impair no social gains and to extend the benefits of social security. The task for today is to preserve the element of competitiveness and at the same time to mitigate its direst consequences. We need above all to learn, and there are some signs that perhaps we are beginning to learn, competitiveness for things other than money and the material rewards; competitiveness in serving others, in sharing, in extending to more and more people the enjoyment of what is good and true and beautiful.

Many Americans have shown the way in these other kinds of competition that are less personally demanding and in the long run far more rewarding. Although he was born to wealth and position, Gifford Pinchot devoted a large part of his life to establishing the idea of conservation and to preserving for future generations part of the heritage of the continent as it was before civilization swept down so much of its natural grandeur. In partnership with Theodore Roosevelt he brought about a radical change in the way Americans thought about their own country.

The field for competition here is so wide that it is in fact unlimited. And the enterprise of the individual, the contribution he makes to society and to his own enrichment, may come to mean, even in the external values of a highly competitive society, much more than the valuation of money or the objects money buys. If this sounds utopian, the only reply is that it must happen, as indeed there are indications it is beginning to happen, if we are to avoid the fate of every other civilization out of the past.

CHAPTER V

The Businessman's Dilemma

BACK IN THE EIGHTEENTH CENTURY John Wesley once expressed what seemed to him a curious dilemma. He said that religion makes a man frugal, and frugality begets wealth. Wealth makes a man indifferent to religion, so it seems that religion destroys itself.

It is a dilemma that has vexed the businessman through the centuries. Perhaps it is not quite so simple as John Wesley formulated it. But it is certainly true that the compulsion of success in business has tended to make a man neglectful of his Christian faith. He finds he must somehow try to reconcile what one observer has described as the impersonal imperative of profit and efficiency with the personal imperative of Christian ethics. This quest—a seeking for some sort of moral equilibrium—arises anew for each generation and each individual. In America the very concept of equilibrium, implying the Greek idea of balance, has somehow seemed alien to our tradition. Its achievement, therefore, has been all the more difficult.

A contemporary of Wesley, John Woolman of New Jersey, sought and found his moral equilibrium. Woolman, a Quaker, made of his business career a continuous struggle to impose his spiritual discoveries on his mercantile store, his tailoring business and his law practice. He believed firmly in the Quaker precept taught by William Penn that merchants should be "tenants of the public." One day, for example, he decided he could no longer write wills transferring slaves. "As writing is a profitable employ," he wrote, "as offending sober people is disagreeable to me, I was straitened in my mind; but . . . I told the man that I believed the practice of continuing slavery to these people was not right, and had a scruple in my mind against doing writings of that kind." Woolman's uneasiness about slavery was to spread to a great many other people during the next hundred years.

But prosperity itself had its moral pitfalls for Woolman. "Having got a considerable shop of goods," he wrote in his journal, "my trade increased every year and the road to large business appeared open, but I felt a stop in my mind . . . The increase in business became my burden; for though my natural inclination was toward merchandise, yet I believed truth required me to live more free from outward cumbers . . . In a while I wholly laid down merchandise . . . I found it good for me to advise poor people to take such things as were most useful, and not costly."

Thus Woolman's searching led to a self-abnegation which eventually carried him right out of the world of business. But for those following a second moral tradition in American business such a course was patently ridiculous. For Cotton Mather, for example, who has been called the American high priest of this second tradition, wealth was a sign of divine favor and its getting was a way of glorifying God. "Sirs," he once declared, "you cannot but acknowledge that it is the Sovereign God who has bestowed upon you the riches which distinguish you." And another time, "I tell you with *Diligence* a man may do marvelous things. *Young* man, work hard while you are *Young*. Let your business engross most of your time . . ." Benjamin Franklin himself was a leading disciple of the

Mather tradition. Though his career was a gloriously varied one he looked upon himself primarily as a business-man. His will began, "I, Benjamin Franklin, Printer . . ." Frugality, diligence, honesty—these were the Puri-tanical virtues which applied to the world of business were well calculated to push a man onward and upward.

During most of the nineteenth century in America these two traditions maintained a healthy tension within the business community. Always dominant was the strict Calvinist devotion to duty and hard work. But underlying this and occasionally cropping to the surface was the tra-dition of Christian sentiment and good works. There were quite a few like John Woolman who found their con-sciences leading them into what appeared unbusinesslike practices. There was Jonas Chickering the piano maker, for example, who said to his debtors, "If you cannot pay me now, pay me when you can; if never able to pay me I shall not trouble you . . ." Business at its best during this period helped create the general ethics of the time.

More than simply a conflict between man's ideals and man's behavior, this dualism can be traced back to a conundrum posed by Christ himself. In the Parable of the Talents Christ taught that each man should be re-warded according to his "good and faithful" services; here lay solid foundations for Mather's emphasis on hard work and wealth-amassing. In the Parable of the Vineyard Christ taught that each worker would be rewarded equally no matter what part of the day he labored; here was a mes-sage which goes beyond socialistic equality. Of course the link between the two parables, frequently overlooked, was the idea that all man's worldly wealth should be held as a stewardship to God.

With Cotton Mather this sense of stewardship was an implied though not always strongly emphasized part of his code of business ethics. But with the great expansion of industrialization toward the latter part of the nineteenth century a neo-Calvinist tradition sprang up which paid scarce heed to stewardship. Some, indeed, tried to formulate a kind of divine right of businessmen, as when George Baer said, "The rights and interests of the laboring man will be protected and cared for—not by the labor agitators, but by the Christian men to whom God in his infinite wisdom has given the control of the property interests of the country . . ." But most men of wealth in Baer's day traced their trusteeship to God very indirectly, finding instead a sanction for their activities in social Darwinism supported by the growing idea of laissez-faire economics.

Fortune magazine has commented that, "By the end of the (nineteenth) century . . . God was no longer in business in any real sense." Such a judgment need not be limited to the so-called "robber barons" who hardly practiced a form of capitalism at all but were, as one observer noted, engaged in juvenile warfare, "small boys joyous in chicanery." Even so conscientious a man as Thomas Mellon of Pittsburgh, though devoting himself assiduously to the maxims he had read in Ben Franklin's "Autobiography," still found it difficult to keep his proportions straight in the post-Civil War era. Owning a great slice of the property of his city, he insisted that he foreclosed properties only of men "weakened by bad habits and extravagant living." But it has been said that there were a great many such weak men in Mellon's eyes.

So it was that the American businessman, entering the Golden Age of American business, seemed to lose the sense of certainty of his own purpose. He had come into power and he had discovered that power corrupts. But more, he had somehow got his means inextricably confused with his ends. He sought wealth, but beyond the limited wants of bodily comfort he had no real sense of why he was seeking it. And while he searched there was built up an accumulated resentment over the abuses he was helping cause. First he was muckraked; later, with the New Deal, he was pretty largely ignored.

A great deal of literature has been devoted to the businessman's quest to find himself. Much of it has been in a satirical vein, written by outsiders who could not really be sure what was going on inside the businessman. Last year a businessman turned novelist to write his own account. The book, "Executive Suite" by Cameron Hawley, has a simple plot. The President of Tredway Furniture Company dies suddenly without having indicated which of his vice-presidents he has marked for the succession. The story concerns the next twenty-four hours and the struggle for power that goes on within that group.

But more than simply an account of a power struggle, it is a story of the differing values which the various men bring to the company. The choice narrows down to two men. Loren P. Shaw, the Comptroller, views the Presidency as primarily a financial responsibility. As agent for the stockholders he will dedicate himself to increased profits and to such accounting procedures, etc., as will make a sound financial institution of the business. His leading competitor, Don Walling, finds in the Tredway Corporation a greater challenge.

At the critical gathering when the decision is reached Walling and Shaw become involved in a discussion of what can be the incentive of a corporation chief executive. Shaw mentions that $60,000 a year might be considered something of an incentive. To which Walling replies, "Do you really think that a man of that caliber would be willing to sell his life for money—for what would be left out of $60,000 a year after taxes?"

"We have to keep this company *alive*," he continues. "That's the important thing—and a company is like a man. No man can work for money alone. It isn't enough. You starve his soul when you try it—and you can starve a company to death in the same way. Yes, I know—some-

times our men in the factories give us the impression that
all they want is another raise in wages—and then another
and another and another. They make us think that getting more money is all that matters to them. But can we
blame them for that? God knows, we've done our best to
try to make them believe that money is the only measure
of accomplishment that matters to us."

That something a company has to have, according to
Walling, is pride. "A company is like an army—it fights
on its pride," he says. "You can't win wars with pay
checks. In all the history of the world there's never been
a great army of mercenaries. You can't pay a man enough
to make him lay down his life. He wants more than
money."

So Walling gets the job and the promise he makes his
fellow executives is a specific one. "We haven't even
started to grow!" he exults. "Suppose we get 15 per cent of
the total—and why not? It's been done in a dozen industries. Fifteen per cent and the Tredway Corporation will
be five times as big as it is today. All right, I know it hasn't
been done before in the furniture business, but does that
mean we can't do it? No—because that's exactly what we
are going to do!"

Don Walling and Tredway Corporation presumably
find their salvation for the time at least in greater productivity. This "Gospel of Production," as *Fortune* calls it,
has played a large part in stimulating the creative genius
of the American businessman. Its ark was the machine;
its high priest Henry Ford. Far more than profits Ford
wanted to make motor cars and he wanted to make them
better and cheaper. When stockholders brought suit
against him in 1916 to compel him to cut a melon he had
earmarked for a price-cut from $440 to $360 for his car,
Ford explained, "We cut prices and are now clearing $2
million to $2,500,000 a month, which is all any firm ought
to make—maybe more—unless the money is to be used for

expansion. I have been fighting to hold income down right along." The court sternly reprimanded Ford for his neglect of the shareholders, but failed to find a way to prevent such behavior.

The convenient and yet the disturbing thing about the Gospel of Production was that it had a bread-upon-the-waters twist to it. By lowering prices and increasing production Ford and others discovered that they made greater profits and grew ever bigger. They also accumulated tremendous economic power which permitted them to do pretty much as they wished. Thus in finding a sense of meaning for himself Ford handed to his successors even more complex problems to be solved in their own search. They had to reconcile their personal ethics with the impersonal imperatives of great business that no longer played its traditional competitive role in the market place.

Let us consider an indictment made against giant business by a big businessman of recent times. In 1935 Theodore Quinn, son of a working man, had by means of steadfast devotion to his job arrived at the position of Vice President of the huge General Electric Company. The President, Gerard Swope, had told him that before many more years Quinn would be his successor. Yet Theodore Quinn, still in his early forties, handed in his resignation. His explanation: "I began to realize that I was serving no socially worthwhile purpose in helping a giant to become even bigger."

A part of Quinn's indictment as recounted in his recent book "Giant Business" is leveled against this growth for growth's sake. His villains are the 58 billionaire corporations which he feels are throttling the private enterprise system in America. It is intolerable, he charges, that the condition should exist whereby the "monster" corporations have the power to let others live by tolerance only. He paints a gloomy picture of thousands of small subcontractors and distributors existing in a state of peonage to big business, fearful lest at any time they be cut off and annihilated.

But Theodore Quinn's principal indictment is against what he believes giant corporate business has done to the individuals inside it. He contrasts the great self-reliance and ambition of the young man of his own generation with the aspirations of the young men entering the vast bureaucracy of business today. He compares the warm humanity of some of the smaller business leaders he used to know with the impersonality—the subordination and the regimentation—that he believes characterizes the giant corporations which swallowed them up. There is, he maintains, utter inhumanity of man toward man when the corporate interest is involved.

What is the element that has got lost along the way? Quinn believes it is, "Living out one's life in the company of people who really know each other, deep down, and who, living in one community, usefully face together social discipline, integration, and maturity. The absorption of human lives in industrial centralization, and in the techniques of less responsible mass movements, belittles the individual. The loss of conscience, mutual respect, consideration and wholesome humanity becomes greater than any possible gain."

In contrast to the dark-toned portrait of the new American businessman painted by Theodore Quinn, others have used more roseate hues. *Fortune* magazine, for example, over the past few years has devoted itself to an effort to capture his true features. Where Quinn could only despair, *Fortune* and its writers find abundant grounds for hope. They describe the passing of the industrial tycoon, who ruled with lust for power and who left to his declining years the good works that he so studiedly neglected while he was in business. In his stead has come the "manager," a man of technical accomplishment, though not primarily a technician, whose major task is to weigh the competing demands of the stockholder, the worker, and the consumer. "The new manager was not, after all, expected to run the show," according to *Fortune*. "He was expected to fuse the judgments of other managers and keep the company in balance. He was expected to be receptive." Or, in the words of Frank Abrams, Chairman of the Board of Standard Oil Company (New Jersey), the job of management is to maintain "an equitable and working balance among the claims of the various directly interested groups."

According to a survey which *Fortune* made of the top 900 executives of the 300 biggest industrial companies, railroads, and utilities, the transition from first-generation to second-generation management was essentially a salesman's job. For more than one-third of the younger executives, experience in sales had led them to the top. They had gained, according to *Fortune,* a capacity for taking a broad view of company activities, and an ability to get along with people.

The managers of the big company, working together in the endless committee and board meetings, while not perhaps steadfastly pursuing the Quaker goal of service to God, have at least adapted the Quaker tradition of seeking to achieve a "sense of the meeting." And it is the factors taken into account in achieving that "sense of the meeting" which give the self-proclaimed boosters for the new businessman a great deal of their enthusiasm. No longer is there simply a dry statistical analysis of the profit and loss sheet. "At least half of our time is taken up with discussing the repercussions of what we propose to do," one executive has remarked. "And this is what the boys who write the books call the managerial revolution."

What are some of these new factors? William J. Miller, writing in *Time* Magazine, discusses the growth of "Human Relations" which he says is a new art bringing a revolution to industry. He harks back to the time when Frederick Winslow Taylor increased production by rationalizing it, a process which carried to its ultimate conclusion turned the factory worker into little more than the cog so effectively satirized by Charlie Chaplin. But from the pioneering works of Elton Mayo industry has at last discovered that it can also increase production by humanizing it. As a result of elaborately scientific investigations made by Mayo at such factories as the Hawthorne Works of Western Electric near Chicago, management has come to the absurdly simple conclusion that every worker likes to feel his work important. And he will work harder if he feels that way! That discovery, firmly based on self-interest, has been having a tremendous impact on the modern businessman. Chairman Clarence Francis of General Foods, for example, has been prompted to declare: "You can buy a man's time, you can buy a man's physical presence at a given place; you can even buy a measured number of skilled muscular actions per hour a day. But you cannot buy enthusiasm; you cannot buy initiative; you cannot buy loyalty; you cannot buy the devotion of heart, mind, and soul. You have to earn these things . . ."

So it would seem that self-interest has led the businessman toward many of the same goals in employee relations that those advocating the *service* principle have set themselves. Admittedly, this victory has been hard won and its implications have yet to be carried to their logical conclusions throughout the business world. Still, a start has been made, insist the boosters. *Fortune* feels inspired to write a glowing article praising the formerly much-condemned Standard Oil of New Jersey, with its "Advisory Committee on Human Relations"; and its subsidiary Esso Standard, which offers practically cradle-to-the-grave security to its workers.

The impact of this business humanity has at times extended beyond the walls of the factory to have a humanizing influence on the entire community. A few years ago, for example, the Calumet and Hecla Consolidated Copper Company set out to select a southern city as the location for a large plant for its Wolverine Tube Division. Decatur, Alabama, was the site finally chosen, much to the disappointment of several other candidates including a city in Mississippi which had offered considerable inducement in the way of subsidies. When this latter city wanted to know why it was not chosen, an official of Calumet and Hecla, H. Y. Bassett, prepared a short article entitled "What Does Industry Expect of a Community?" To the surprise of many who had believed that cheap unorganized labor was one of the South's invaluable commodities, Bassett argued exactly the opposite. "Progressive managements," he wrote, "have no quarrel with unions, but on the contrary feel that they have a place in the present day world of business . . . That being so it would not be good judgment to locate in a town where the practices are contrary to those carried on by that management in its other existing plants." Furthermore, Bassett pointed out that modern management is interested in the public school system, the recreation facilities, and all the other factors in a community which are vital to its employees. "This," he said, "is not a matter of philanthropy, but of good business practice . . . And these matters are of far more importance to a plant in the long run than any subsidy of a more material sort which a community may offer."

Along with that growing sense of community responsibility, the community in turn has come to have a broader concept of the responsibility of business. In 1948, for example, when Textron suddenly announced its intention to close its Nashua, N. H. mills with the loss of 3500 jobs there was immediate and forceful public reaction; Senator Tobey of New Hampshire instituted hearings on the matter. As a result Roy Little, head of Textron, was obliged to adopt a compromise plan which would lessen the immediate impact on the community. As one observer commented, "There is little doubt that in the long run the city of Nashua will have a sounder economic base as a result of the closing. The company's obligation to the city is to see how much that long run can be shortened."

These and countless other examples add up to the transformation of the American businessman in the eyes of his favorable critics. There is still another part of the picture which must be sketched in. It is that tremendous amount of organized community and philanthropic activities which have earned him the title of "the busy, busy citizen." Undoubtedly the 200,000 such groups holding more than 17,000 state and national conventions a year play a fundamental part in the life of America. By their good works they represent a kind of third force in the American power system distinct from the traditional political and economic power systems. Although there is no longer the possibility that a Rockefeller can contribute three-quarters of a billion dollars to philanthropic activities, the individual businessman and his wife, working in their various groups, help to raise some three billion annually for philanthropy. In the Community Chest, the Red Cross, the local Lions or Rotary Club, the businessman discovers a fuller meaning for himself than he finds in his strictly work-a-day activity.

Giving by corporations themselves has come to play an ever-increasing part in national good works. In 1949 over $223,000,000 came from this source. As if to reconcile the conflict of self-interest with community service, Congress in 1935 adopted a provision whereby a corporation could deduct five per cent of its net earning from taxable income if contributed for educational, scientific, and welfare purposes. When in 1951 the National Planning Associa-

tion published a brief report, "The Five Per Cent," showing that because of high corporate taxation the government was actually subsidizing business to engage in
philanthropy, the booklet immediately became a best
seller. Subsequently the NPA has published a "Manual
of Corporate Giving," designed to answer the questions
of businessmen who wish to start a sensible program of
corporate giving. According to estimates there is a potential goal of one-to-two billion dollars a year which could
fall in this category—an amount which if properly used
could play a great part in supplanting government welfare activities in the nation.

All the factors, actual and potential, which have been
enumerated above have earned the glowing tributes paid
to a "transformed" American capitalism, led by the
"managerial" businessman, espousing a "gospel of service." "The larger corporation," wrote one optimistic
observer, "is becoming one of free society's major instru-
ments of economic justice." Business leaders such as Frank
Abrams, Philip Reed, and others have not infrequently
been handed the accolade of "industrial statesmen." For
John Knox Jessup, Chairman of the Editorial Board of
Fortune, American business has outraced the imagination
of its utopian critics, the socialists. "Our business civilization," he writes, "has not only contradicted their prophe-
sies, but exhausted their dreams." Jessup is prompted to
advocate a new role for the corporation—something approaching a political role. He feels that it can supplant
the archaic system of states as a focal point of self-government, and thereby fill the vacuum now existing in the
federal republic. As reasons for this he cites the fact that
the corporation has fast been taking on new social responsibilities, that it has in fact become a sort of welfare
community.

For Jessup this does not mean that the businessman
must become a professional politician. "The manager's

political function as I see it," he writes, "is simply to make his corporation successful. It is to keep proving in the future what he has already begun to prove; namely, that the corporation is a new, vital kind of commonwealth, within which individual citizens can work to produce wealth and harmony and to share rewards in a spirit of practical justice. As chief of this little commonwealth, the manager has the political job of keeping all his constituents reasonably happy in that part of their lives which relates to work."

Thus in one mighty leap Jessup would hurdle the boundaries which divide the economic and the political power systems of the country. Indeed, he argues that these boundaries have already been downtrodden. "Any President who wants to run a country," he observes, "depends on the corporation at least as much as—probably more than—the corporation depends on him. His dependence is not unlike that of King John on the landed barons of Runnymede, where Magna Carta was born."

There are few who would agree with such exaggerated conclusions or would welcome the feudal type of society that Jessup predicts. Yet his analysis does serve to raise some of the more serious questions that occur to anyone examining the implications of the movement toward a corporate welfare community. If a welfare state can be termed oppressive to individual freedom, how much less oppressive is a welfare corporation upon whose social security system the individual comes to have ever greater dependence? How does he maintain his traditional freedom of movement between jobs or communities? What, too, is to happen to those whose jobs lie outside the boundaries of the large corporations?

These questions in turn lead to the larger questions that occur when one contemplates a genuine conflict of interest between the corporate good and the community good. How effective, for example, would the "new manager" be in the event of a marked recession or even depression in the economy? In late 1946 some 15,000 leading business executives were asked if they expected an "extended major depression with large-scale unemployment in the next ten years." Fifty-eight per cent of those replying (in confidence) said they did. Of the remainder, only twenty-eight per cent said no. Yet it is doubtful if the individual businessman or the individual corporation could take the kind of remedial steps that would be necessary to ameliorate and overcome the effect of large-scale depression. The American businessman, in his more sober moments, realizes this fact. As the official autobiography of DuPont stated so eloquently in describing the problems which have faced that giant corporation during its 150-year history, "The problems of 1952 are not so clearly defined. For the most part these are not within DuPont jurisdiction—they reflect the broad social and economic issues of the times."

While Jessup sees only the expanding social capacity of the large corporation, Theodore Quinn sees its social and economic dependency. Quinn argues that General Motors, regardless of how badly it might be operated, could no more be allowed to fail than we can contemplate the failure of Michigan, Colorado, or Virginia. Similarly, he says, we can no longer afford the failure of Standard Oil of New Jersey, Chase National Bank, or American Telephone and Telegraph. Instead of alleviating the need for government, Quinn finds that this only increases that need. He envisages a time when, if the failure of any of these giant corporations were in prospect, the government might have to step in and take over directly. The growth of large-scale corporate enterprise presents for Quinn the threat of corporative government, one brand of collectivism. Whether his fears are overwrought or not, the criticism he poses to Jessup's notion of a political role for corporations seems devastating. Cor-

porate business, whose management is self-elected and for
the most part self-perpetuating, can never be allowed to
usurp the role of the political system responsible to the
more general needs of the people.

Howard R. Bowen, in his book "Social Responsibilities
of the Businessman," one volume of the series on Ethics
and Economic Life, has made a systematic study of the
businessman's concept of his social responsibilities. He
finds, gratifyingly, that today's businessmen are in fact
more concerned than were their predecessors about this social responsibility. The reason is threefold: They have
been forced to be more concerned, they have been persuad-
ed to be more concerned, and, owing largely to the separation of ownership and control in the large corporations,
conditions have been favorable to the development of this
concern.

One has only to read the speeches being made by today's
businessmen to find a constant articulation of this concern. Two instances will serve to show the trend:

"It seems to me only too obvious that the survival
of private enterprise requires that private enterprise
act to maintain a productive and equitable relation
among these three elements: the individual's right to
and social necessity for profits; the economic and human aspirations of all workers; and the public's demand for an abundance of goods at low cost. The
alternative is plainly intensified industrial conflict
followed by increased government regulation enforced by an impatient public." [1]

"An active social conscience . . . and individual
recognition of social responsibilities will compel us,
as individuals, to test every managerial practice, measure every policy by a single yardstick. Not 'what does

[1] Frank W. Pierce, director of the Standard Oil Company (New
Jersey).

it mean for me' but rather 'what will this mean to my workers as people, to my customers, to my suppliers, to my stockholders, to the community in which my plant is located, to my government, to the industry of which I am a part, to the economy as a whole?' " [2]

At Harvard University no one laughs any longer when the candidates for the Master's degree from the Business School are welcomed into the "oldest of the arts and youngest of the professions." More and more the concept has grown up in the American business community of the professional responsibility of the businessman. This growing awareness is of enormous significance.

One evidence of the fact that the businessman is now aware of the social effect of his decisions may be seen in the growth of the huge public relations industry superimposed on the industrial life of the nation. Public relations clarifies for the businessman the moral issue confronting him. Shall his public relations be honest or dishonest? Just as nineteenth-century laissez-faire business ruled out the fraudulent product in its system of ethics, so twentieth-century business ethics should not permit fraudulent public relations. As Bowen points out, one strong reservation held by many serious students of modern business arises from a suspicion that the doctrine of social responsibility espoused by businessmen is merely a propaganda device by which they hope to maintain power. There are notable skeptics on this score as, for example, Dr. Edwin C. Nourse, former chairman of the President's Council of Economic Advisers, who has remarked that the trusteeship concept held by many businessmen "has a fine baronial flavor generously tinctured with *noblesse oblige.*"

Part of this skepticism undoubtedly stems from the phoniness of the public relations conducted by some busi-

2 Morris Sayre, president of the Corn Products Refining Company.

nesses. Part, too, arises from the advertising industry which has grown to such fantastic heights in the modern business system. The citizen knows that a great part of the advertising campaign conducted for his purchasing dollar is based on an attempt to sell without very much regard for the truth. He buys a cigarette which the movie star or the athlete purports to find most satisfying, but he maintains a cynical attitude just the same. His cynicism is apt to extend to the business ethics which will countenance such advertising.

For the businessman, the answer to this lies over and beyond the science of public relations. It alone, any more than the gospel of productivity, pride of service, or any other single factor, cannot provide for him the lasting incentive—the deeper meaning. David Riesman in "The Lonely Crowd" has described eloquently the plight of the "other directed" person, guided radar-like by the desire to get along with those around him. As Riesman makes clear, little is gained in moving from a society trusting blindly in Adam Smith's "unseen hand" to a society presided over by the "glad hand." In such a society the businessman would find little to guide him when confronted by a true moral issue—when, for instance, self-interest and social interest are in direct conflict and cannot be reconciled by a five per cent tax deduction or when "human relations" does not necessarily point the way to stepped-up production.

CHAPTER VI

Free Enterprise—Fact and Fantasy

TAWNEY, describing the gradual breakdown of the ecclesiastical authority in the Middle Ages, commented:

"With the expansion of finance and international trade in the sixteenth century, it was this problem which faced the Church: Granted that I should love my neighbor as myself, the questions which, under modern conditions of large-scale organization, remain for solution are, Who precisely *is* my neighbor? and, How exactly am I to make my love for him effective in practice? . . . In an age of impersonal finance, world-markets, and a capitalist organization of industry, its traditional social doctrines had no specific to offer, and were merely repeated, when, in order to be effective, they should have been thought out again from the beginning and formulated in new and living terms."

One notes a startling parallelism of thought in the report in 1939 prepared by the Temporary National Economic Committee which had been set up to probe some of the basic problems vexing twentieth-century America:

"The upheaval in which this generation is caught proceeds from the failure of leadership, here and throughout the world, to comprehend that the nineteenth century is as completely an era of the past as

is the eighteenth. . . . The sort of competition
of which most observers seem to think when they
are considering the chaotic conditions which en-
mesh us is the competition of individuals, using the
tools and working within the limitations of the last
century. The record of this Committee is full of comments by some of the wisest observers who came
before us, in which the personal pronouns 'he' and
'him' were used to designate the units of modern
competition although, as a matter of fact, the economic behavior of individual competitors is no part
of our problem. What we are concerned with is the
behavior of the huge collective groups which use
the tools of the twentieth century and are not ham-
pered by any of the limitations of the nineteenth
century which retained the business of that era
within local boundaries and to the jurisdiction of
local governments."

There, stated succinctly if a bit pessimistically, is the
problem which has troubled a great many Americans.
The statistics of the situation can be stated fairly simply:
in a brief fifty-year span the nation's population has increased by approximately 90 percent; yet, during that
same time span its physical volume of manufacturing production has increased by 540 per cent, or six times as much.

No one, of course, has an unkind word to say about
such a fantastic jump in productivity, but a number have
looked searchingly at what was happening to the system
itself during this period of well-nigh hyperthyroid
growth. Was the classic model of Adam Smith in which
the wheels, all of them fairly small wheels, turned and
meshed to maintain an optimum state of balance, still
valid? Obviously the requirement, if it was a requirement,
of small size no longer held good. Mid-twentieth-century
America was an economy of very big wheels interspersed

with little ones. The biggest 200 employers alone in terms of assets held about 40 per cent of all corporate assets and between one-fourth and one-fifth of total national income-yielding wealth. They accounted for one-eighth of the total civilian labor force and one-fifth of all employees of private businesses outside of agriculture. Obviously, this was a market place in which giants abounded—not the Adam Smith market place in which an unlimited number of small producers dealt freely and competitively with one another.

But this raised further questions for the serious student of the American economy: Were there limits to the growth of bigness or was a galloping concentration taking over the American economy? Did this bigness mean the end of free enterprise which was basic to the Adam Smith system? Finally, was there any longer an "unseen hand" to maintain an optimum condition in the economy?

Surprisingly, despite the growth of accounting proficiency, the statistics seem to tell a different story to different people. They are so inconclusive that Edward S. Mason, Professor of Economics at Harvard, remarked in 1952: "We don't know whether concentration is increasing, decreasing, or standing pat. In the manufacturing sector of the economy we don't know whether the hundred largest firms have a larger or smaller per cent of total assets than the largest hundred did fifty or sixty years ago." The nature of the mystery is that while big business has vastly grown in the economy, the economy itself has grown on an equally vast scale. While there are more big businesses—and bigger big businesses—today than ever before, there are also more small businesses (and bigger small businesses).

But if concentration is not a galloping phenomenon on the American scene a good many people have acted as if they thought it were. As far back as the spring of 1901 when the news broke that J. Pierpont Morgan had formed the U. S. Steel Corporation, such a conservative as President Hadley of Yale was provoked to exclaim that unless some way could be found to restrict such trusts, there would be "an emperor in Washington within twenty-five years." In 1932, two economists, Adolf A. Berle Jr., and Gardiner Means, sounded an alarm over the growth of corporate power which was heard all the more widely because the nation found itself in the depths of its worst depression. In "The Modern Corporation and Private Property," Berle and Means pointed out that since 1909 the 200 largest industrial corporations had been growing at a rate which, if continued, would mean that by 1950 they would hold between seventy and eighty-five per cent of all corporate wealth.

In 1948, despite the obvious failure of the Berle and Means prediction, the Federal Trade Commission again voiced grave fears over corporate growth in its report to the House Judiciary Committee headed by Congressman Emanuel Celler:

> "No great stretch of the imagination is required to foresee that if nothing is done to check the growth in concentration, either the giant corporations will ultimately take over the country, or the government will be impelled to step in and impose some form of direct regulation in the public interest. In either event, collectivism will have triumphed over free enterprise. . ."

Those who sought to allay the fear of galloping concentration could muster an impressive set of their own statistics. They have pointed out that there has been a sharp decline of the classic monopolies, nearly every one of which—steel, oil, tobacco, copper refining, sugar, rubber, cans, farm machinery, aluminum—has suffered at least a halving of its market share over the past fifty years. The number of separate businesses has more than kept up with the population. In 1900 Dun & Bradstreet listed 1,170,000 businesses in the U. S., or almost fifteen and a half per thousand persons; in 1950 it listed 2,020,000 or slightly over eighteen per thousand. In 1953 in a *Fortune* article entitled "Big Business in a Competitive Society," A. D. H. Kaplan and Alfred E. Kahn tried once and for all to quiet the fears raised by the earlier Berle and Means study. They report that, excluding the railroads and public utilities, the corporate assets of the remaining 106 largest industrials surveyed by Berle and Means declined from about thirty per cent of the nation's total in 1929 to not quite twenty-seven per cent in 1948. The 100 largest industrials in 1948, they estimate, accounted for approximately twelve per cent of all income originating in American private business. A large chunk, they agree, but nothing approaching the frightening proportions predicted by Berle and Means.

But those who warned against the sweeping growth of bigness might well argue that they have not been refuted simply by a parade of statistics. In part they could point to the results achieved by their warnings—the recurrent legal attack on monopoly and unfair trade practices. There had been Teddy Roosevelt's noisy crusade against the trusts, followed by the quieter and more effective work of William Howard Taft and Woodrow Wilson; after the giddy forgetfulness of the 'twenties, and after the ill-fated experiment with the NRA, another Roosevelt Administration initiated an even greater effort to beat down restraints to the freely competitive economy. No one can calculate the effect of what Justice Holmes once called the "brooding omnipresence" of the antitrust laws. It was a Cabinet member of the new Republican Administration, Attorney General Herbert Brownell, who declared recently that these laws are "a part of the warp and woof of our economic life."

The war against bigness was not limited exclusively to a percentagewise effort to reduce monopolistic enterprise in America. More than that it was a frontal onslaught against the undesirable conditions of American economic life that seemed to be part and parcel of this bigness. It was stimulated by the fear of what would happen to the individual in America as a result of organizational giantism. As the TNEC Report concluded, "Democracy, which surely comprehends economic as well as political freedom for the natural person, cannot endure when the natural person cannot shape the policies and the activities of the collective agencies which control all the materials of his economic life. The American ideal of living has not changed, but the forms of our economic life have changed and most radically. The new forms of industrial organization are such that competition has become a vastly more difficult status to maintain and the American ideal of free living for people is not nearly so easy of achievement as before organizations superseded men in the economy."

One of the earlier and more eloquent condemners of this moral wrongness of bigness was Louis Brandeis, whose skill as a legal advocate and warmth as a humanitarian had gained him widespread prominence long before he reached the eminence of the Supreme Court bench. For Brandeis the uncontrolled power which was the inevitable companion of bigness contained a curse. "The successful, the powerful trusts, have created conditions absolutely inconsistent with these—America's—industrial and social needs," he wrote in 1912. "It may be true that as a legal proposition mere size is not a crime, but mere size may become an industrial and social menace, because it frequently creates as against possible competitors and as against the employees conditions of such gross inequality, as to imperil the welfare of the employees and of the industry." Brandeis could belittle the argument that bigness brought about increased efficiency.

"Whenever trusts have developed efficiency," he wrote, "their fruits have been absorbed almost wholly by the trusts themselves. From such efficiency as they have developed, the community has gained substantially nothing."

Brandeis won a deep response from the American people when he inveighed against the "soulless corporation" and buttressed his argument with the statistical evidence that a worker in the steel industry had to labor 365 days a year twelve hours a day to earn a wage which fell just short of bare subsistence income. In the steel industry, Brandeis pointed out, there were only two holidays during the year, Christmas and the Fourth of July. And for those working in the shriveling heat of the blast furnaces even these holidays were denied. "Think of that situation," he wrote, "side by side with the enormous profits taken from the American people to be distributed among stockholders of the Steel Trust." The alternatives, he said: "Either political liberty will be extinguished or industrial liberty must be restored."

It is a fascinating experience to read side by side with Brandeis' "Curse of Bigness" a book written in 1953 by David Lilienthal entitled "Big Business: A New Era." Lilienthal, formerly head of TVA and later Chairman of the Atomic Energy Commission has, like Brandeis, achieved wide renown as an articulator of the American dream. While Brandeis might be called the apostle of industrial unrest, Lilienthal in his recent book could just as aptly be called the apostle of industrial complacency. Brandeis wrote at a time when the unparalleled profits of big corporations stood in glaring contrast to the miserable conditions of the working man. Lilienthal writes in an era when the wage and working conditions of at least the organized laborer have kept close step with those profits. For Lilienthal, bigness has lost its curse.

Essentially, Lilienthal sketches a picture of what might

be called "housebroken" big business. He speaks of the watering down of corporate power with the rise of the managerial class to take the place of the crude, undisciplined industrial tycoons of earlier days. He describes the growth of big labor, big agriculture, and, indeed, big buyers to offset the economic power of the big manufacturer. He also indicates that the rise of big government had served as an effective restraint and counterbalance to the power of big business.

These factors and others contribute to what Lilienthal calls "the new competition"—a competition which is a far cry from that competitive economy envisaged by Adam Smith. Basically a competition among giants, it is measured not in the prices charged in the market place but in various other ways. The competition of alternative products is one form of this "new competition" Lilienthal describes. If copper is overpriced, for example, aluminum moves in to take its place in the economy. There is the competition of research as the manufacturer strives to find ways to improve the product which he offers in the market. Lilienthal points to competition within a single company as, for example, the Chevrolet division of General Motors actively pitted against the Pontiac division; the Oldsmobile versus the Buick. There is, likewise, a competition or threat of competition between supplier and manufacturer, between wholesaler and retailer. General Motors will hold down prices in the steel industry by threatening to acquire its own steel production facilities. Sears Roebuck and the A&P maintain a similar competitive threat over the heads of the various manufacturers.

As a result, productivity, according to Lilienthal, has taken the place of price as the chief measuring rod of the competitive economy—productivity on so great a scale that the traditional economic concept of scarcity is no longer a valid one. The job now is how best to distribute the abundance which American enterprise has made available. If in providing for this distribution there is no longer the price competition of olden days, this, he claims, is not a total loss.

Lilienthal calls for a new "affirmative" belief in bigness. He decries what he terms the "double negative" of our antitrust legislation. Instead he urges a belief in the worth of bigness measured in positive terms—by its provision of greater freedom of choice for the consumer, by its addition to productivity per unit of dollar and human energy expended, by its contribution to constructive labor-management relations, by its addition to the greater economic stability of the nation, and finally by its resiliency in meeting the changing needs of our economy.

It is possible that Lilienthal's hymn to bigness may in future—possibly less prosperous—years seem overly eulogistic. One can imagine that in a time of severe depression it could be echoed with the same sarcasm as was Herbert Hoover's famous phrase of the optimistic 'twenties, "The slogan of progress is changing from the full dinner pail to the full garage." Theodore Quinn, whom we mentioned in Chapter V, takes issue with Lilienthal generally and specifically in the case of General Motors. He points out, for example, that G.M. used power and influence to get a lion's share of steel in the years of postwar shortage in order to take over a great number of stove and range manufacturing companies. Quinn doesn't believe this expansion for the pure sake of expansion was healthy for G.M. or for the economy.

Whether one agrees with Lilienthal or not, he has made a contribution to the quest for a new model to replace the obviously outmoded Adam Smith version of a free enterprise economy. Others have joined in the quest, classifying their findings as "the new capitalism," "workable competition," "managementism," etc. Perhaps the most interesting among the searchers has been John Kenneth Galbraith, Professor of Economics at Harvard University, who in his book, "American Capitalism," published in 1952, discards the notion that there must be a new definition anyway. The time has come, says Galbraith, to call a spade a spade and to cast out "this preoccupation with competition." He serves up in its stead what he calls "the concept of countervailing power."

Unlike competition among sellers in the Adam Smith sense, Galbraith's countervailing power appears as a force not on the same side but on the opposite side of the market from the producer. *Countervailing* power, which he distinguishes from the *original* power of the producer, is held by the large buyer, by the organized labor union, and, in fact, by the government. In each case, according to Galbraith, this countervailing power serves to hold private economic power of the big businessman in check and therefore affords a substitute for a free competition which no longer exists. Equally important, this countervailing power, says Galbraith, is stimulated by the existence of the original economic power and has what might be called a "self-generating force."

This last, if true, is of signal significance because it serves in a way to replace the "unseen hand" of the Adam Smith economy which brought order to the market place. It contributes to the economic picture a sense of stability which has been lacking so long as no one could discover a self-discipline in the new economy. The job of government, for instance, takes on more manageable proportions if, according to Galbraith's theory, it must merely buttress and supplement the operation of countervailing power. Ethics, too, is not strained to the breaking point if there is a certain power equilibrium inherent in the economy which does not leave everything to the individual mores of the big businessman, the big labor leader, or the big government official. This last has an enormous importance for those who are deeply disturbed by the growth of arbitrary power in the hands of the managers. But the Galbraith model has two serious flaws, pointed out by the author himself. The first is that it does not work with any degree of efficiency in a period of continuing inflation. In such a period rather than balancing out—countervailing power versus original power—they tend to supplement one another in the drive for higher prices and higher wages. Thus they worsen rather than correct the inflationary tendencies. Nor does government itself seem to have the moral stamina during inflationary periods to carry out the policies of high taxation and low spending which are required. When the situation is further complicated by the necessity for huge military expenditures, in the words of the author, "the whole structure of countervailing power in the economy dissolves."

A second flaw in the operation of his model, as seen by Galbraith, is that those lacking ability to organize for their own good are not likely to fare very well under the system of countervailing power. Galbraith points to the Farm Security Administration which was set up during the 'thirties to help low-income and tenant farmers but which petered out because these groups were too weak to defend in Congress and before the public these efforts being made in their behalf. "Support to countervailing power is not endowed *ad hoc* by government," says Galbraith. "It must be sought." This raises a whole series of problems which have long troubled the Christian concerned for the fate of the underdog in society. Galbraith's model of countervailing power, just as the classic Adam Smith model, fails to offer a ready answer to the underdog's dilemma. And this time the underdog may not be simply those who are poor in spirit and competitive zeal, but whole segments of society, including white-collar workers, school teachers, and the civil servants, who are not able to organize in their own interest. Their relative economic standing in a dynamic economy is likely to become progressively worse as the more organized working groups push for better wages.

An easy answer to such a dilemma, however, is not the only thing to be sought. Perhaps it is a good beginning if we come to understand more clearly the nature of the economy in which we live, and if we cast aside outmoded ideas based on long defunct economic models. To cling to the over-simplified version of Adam Smith which has been handed down through the centuries is no more realistic in mid-twentieth century America than to accept the dogmatic class struggle theory of Karl Marx. Marx based his philosophy on the fatalistic assumption that the defects of capitalism are above the will of men to affect them. He predicted the breakdown and overthrow of the American capitalistic system as an irrevocable course of events. We know how false that prediction has proved to be, founded on its belief in an ever more bitter class struggle. As Clair Wilcox, Professor of Economics at Swarthmore College, has written in the *Harvard Business Review:* "The class struggle in America is not a struggle between the proletariat and the bourgeoisie. It is a struggle between functional groups possessing concentrated power—a struggle to control the products of industry." This was not remotely the kind of struggle envisaged by Karl Marx or his followers.

While America has not even come close to experiencing the Marxian class revolution, one should not underestimate the nature of the revolution that has taken place—a revolution in technology which has brought visible change to the nation's physical landscape; an organizational revolution which has changed fundamentally the life of every citizen. It was to stimulate the thinking about this latter revolution that the series on Ethics included "The Organizational Revolution," a study by Professor Kenneth E. Boulding of the University of Michigan.

Boulding sets out to analyze this tremendous transformation of the American economic and social scene over the past century, from a nation which in 1852 hardly knew the meaning of the corporation, the labor union, and the farm organization, to a nation which is today characterized by large-scale organization. Beyond this, he attempts to analyze some of the ethical questions which have been raised by this organizational revolution.

To explain the growth of large-scale organization, Boulding lays great stress on the technical developments, especially those in the field of communication. Not just the telephone and the telegraph which have made possible the instantaneous transmission of information, but also the IBM machine and the other devices for correlating and assessing knowledge, have permitted a growing spread in organizational hierarchy and therefore ever-larger organizations. There is, Boulding points out, still a *brontosaurus* principle working in organizations which sets the limits of true efficiency. Yet, ever new discoveries of technique have made possible the persistent pushing back of the limits at which the *brontosaurus* principle seems to apply. Modern advertising and public relations, as an example, have opened new vistas for the mid-twentieth century corporation's expansion in the market which the earlier corporation could never have foreseen. As a result, we can have no precise knowledge of the size to which a giant corporation or, for that matter, a giant nationstate may in time extend.

It is Boulding's attention to the ethical questions raised by the organizational revolution which have a special significance to our book. What meaning, for example, in a society dominated by large organization have the Ten Commandments, the last six of which deal with questions of morality involving relations with people and groups no larger than a family and no relations with a circle wider than a neighborhood? Even the first four Commandments are concerned with the intensely personal relationship of an individual with his God. Boulding describes what he calls the "common morality" of our Western culture built up by long testing and accretion in societies where organizations were small and where relationships were on a person-to-person basis. How well can that "common morality" be adapted to fit the needs of America today?

A major ethical dilemma, for example, is raised by the organizational practice of "acting in the name of." Can the individual who permits his organizational representative to speak for him in a whole host of matters make certain that his individual code of ethics is maintained by whoever serves as his spokesman? This is peculiarly a problem of organization within an organization; Boulding cites as urgent the need for greater democracy within organizations as they approach a size in which their power is not held readily in check by competitive organizations.

A second dilemma, according to Boulding, is presented by the two-sidedness of organization. He points out that almost every organization exhibits two faces; a smiling face which it turns toward its members and a frowning face which it turns to the world outside. Its very act of including its members in a spirit of solidarity creates a lack of solidarity with non-members.

How, asks Boulding, can the Christian acting in a world of mutually exclusive and competing organizations maintain the wider Christian fellowship with all mankind and at the same time the inner fellowship of the organization?

"He who loves his enemies betrays his friends,
This surely is not what Jesus intends . . ."
wrote Blake in "The Everlasting Gospel." The dilemma is posed just as graphically for the member of a local corporation or labor union who seeks the broader though

perhaps competitive good of his home-town community or his nation.

The far-reaching impact of this dilemma is presented by Boulding in the predicament of the nation-state, itself a product of the organizational revolution, which is today committed to an ever-increasing expenditure for weapons of war in order to preserve the peace. He contrasts the warfare of modern times in which fifty per cent or more of a nation's economy is dedicated to the military effort with that of earlier days when seldom more than five to ten per cent was so involved. Unless some way can be found to break the vicious circle of preparing to deal death in order to preserve life, says Boulding, organization itself may be the unwitting instrument of man's destruction.

An equally terrifying aspect of organizational growth is what Boulding describes as the "growing efficiency of coercion." The organization, as seen most graphically in the dictator state such as the Soviet Union, has become totally paramount over the individual. Techniques of enforcing obedience through conditioning and fear make all hope of freedom for the individual seemingly remote. The struggle between the unarmed citizens and the Communist police of East Germany afforded a dramatic illustration of this dilemma posed by modern large scale organization.

A central issue remains: how to find for the organization that seed of regeneration which in the individual man makes him a child of God? Boulding professes difficulty finding such regenerative powers. He points particularly to the fundamental lack in the organization of a sense of altruism. Many a man has laid down his life for a higher cause than himself. But where in the history of organizations has one voluntarily laid down its life in the interest of humanity? Must the organization, whether it be a corporation, a labor union, or a nation-state, be the embodiment of the most selfish self-interest of its collective membership?

In a brilliant critique included in Boulding's book, Reinhold Niebuhr, Professor of Applied Christianity at Union Theological Seminary, questions whether Boulding has not been influenced too much by the Platonic concept that "body" or "organization" is evil because it is corruptible in contrast to the incorruptible spirit. He wonders whether this doesn't drive the social philosopher too close to the edge of anarchy.

It is not the "body" which is the adversary of the "spirit," Niebuhr argues. The body can be good or evil just as the spirit can be good and evil. The contest, he declares, is between the spirit of love and the spirit of self-love. For Niebuhr, there is nothing intrinsic in the organizational revolution which poses an insoluble problem to men seeking the good.

But neither would he hold that there is anything automatic in man's search for the good. Before the deep spiritual crisis of our times, it is hard to share David Lilienthal's euphemism that "Individualism has reached a new high point in this machine civilization of ours." Individualism to what purpose, one might ask. Undoubtedly, our machine civilization has brought to a larger number of people greater comfort, education, and leisure time. Business has gone far toward emancipating the worker from the more onerous burdens of business. Yet the thoughtful critic might ask whether this of itself has given new meaning to individualism. Does it alone provide the individual the strength and purpose to meet the very problems posed by this machine civilization? We know there is no turning back. "The aircraft is a symbol of our times," Lord Bilsland, President of the Scottish Council, declared recently. "If it stops, it falls out of the sky and is destroyed." Man must somehow keep that machine aloft; yet he must not destroy himself in the process.

CHAPTER VII

Government and Business—The Uneasy Balance

THE LATE Lord John Maynard Keynes, famous British economist, once remarked that "the ideas of economists and political philosophers, both when they are right and when they are wrong, are more powerful than is commonly understood. . . . Practical men, who believe themselves to be quite exempt from any intellectual influence, are usually the slaves of some defunct economist."

Undoubtedly Keynes meant to include in this category the little group of men in the Kremlin who tried to make a whole people conform to the sterile pronouncements of the Marxist Bible. He might also have been thinking about some of the more devout exponents of "Free Enterprise," who burn candles to Adam Smith and exorcise a governmental devil. He might, for example, have pointed to the propagandists described by William H. Whyte, Jr., in a series of articles in *Fortune* later published in the book "Is Anybody Listening?" Whyte discusses the films put out by Ross Roy, Inc., of Detroit, which purport to show an average guy, Tom Smith, that "mankind for centuries has faced political and economic problems surprisingly similar to our own." Tom learns that while all the ancient Spartans waited behind an Iron Curtain of

Communism, the Athenians foolishly pursued an expensive public works and "Soak the Rich" policy. Rome, he also discovers in the film, went to hell because of socialist planners. Then, there is the NAM comic book called "The Fight for Freedom" in which employees can learn what really caused the Revolution of 1776. It seems that over in London there were those "government planners . . ."

Whyte for one believes that the businessman in America has a very strong case to put before the American people. But he strongly objects to the oversimplified presentation which has been characteristic of so many of the exponents of the private enterprise system. He believes there is a serious danger that the American businessman—and he alone—may fall for his own cliché.

Now Whyte's book was written before the change of national administrations in January 1953, but his critique could well be applied to some of the more extreme interpreters of that change. Take, for example, a speech made by Assistant Secretary of the Department of the Interior, Felix Edgar Wormser, at the Montana School of Mines in June 1953. In the course of it Wormser delivered something of a panegyric to his conception of the unrestrained free enterprise system. Under this system, he declared, the "play of economic forces, as expressed in open market prices, helps to correct any imbalance. Trouble only arises when government steps in and futilely attempts to supplant the function of a free market itself." He cited minerals as an example. "If we preserve our freedom we shall find all the metals and minerals we require because, as scarcities appear, an open market will reflect this condition and prices will rise. Incentives are therefore increased to find more of the product. Consumers are compelled to use less of it. . . . The inescapable truth is that even proud governments have to bow to the dictates of economic law."

Strangely, Wormser cites the example of uranium ore, vitally important to atomic bomb production, to show how the "free market" serves to meet heightened demands. Undoubtedly, economic incentive played a part in increasing production of uranium ore. But it has not been a free market—certainly not in any Adam Smith sense—which determined the price. When one buyer, in this case the government, largely dominates the whole outlet for a product, the play of the market place has little self-regulating effect.

The dilemma in which Wormser finds himself is not limited to uranium ore production. While chastising what he calls the "alien" philosophy which has overtaken government, he pauses to pay tribute to a bureau that "typifies government service to the citizens at its best . . . the U. S. Bureau of Mines." Yet he cannot help but be aware, since the Bureau of Mines comes under his official jurisdiction, of its role in an operation that represents governmental involvement in business to the nth degree. By the terms of the Interstate Oil Compact, the Bureau of Mines estimates American consumption requirements for oil, and the great oil-producing states allocate production to fit those specifications. The "Connally Hot Oil Act" makes shipment of unallocated oil a criminal offense. And this scheme was worked out in the main by the oil industry itself!

Taking note of this sort of thing, one critic recently observed that while American businessmen have inveighed against the "planned economy" they have planned the economies of their own industries wherever they could and when necessary invoked government intervention to help them do it. Still the myth of unfettered free enterprise dies hard. To many of those enjoying the return of a Republican Administration in 1953 after twenty long years, the prospects were giddy indeed. They spoke of freeing the free enterprise system, restoring the normal working of the market place, permitting the interest rate to regain its natural level, and above all "obeying the dictates of economic law." Even the new cabinet heads on taking office dutifully paid their respects to the natural law theory. Secretary of Commerce Sinclair Weeks declared "Together we're going to give private enterprise a chance to prove what it can really do for America when it is unshackled and encouraged." Secretary of the Treasury George M. Humphrey: "We are in good hands as long as the great American consumer is free from artificial restraint and can freely decide what he will buy, when he will buy, and what prices he is willing to pay." Secretary of Agriculture Ezra Taft Benson: "The farmer asks for, and should have, a fair chance to make his own way in a field of fair competition." And Assistant Secretary Wormser, with a reckless disregard for his Adam Smith heritage, asserted: "For thousands of years nothing like this basic doctrine of freedom of the market place occurred anywhere on earth."

A part of this could be attributed to the *joie de vivre* of the new politicians who did not feel quite the same compulsion to be precise as the social scientist. In part, too, it was a reaction against what many regarded as an overconcentration of activity in the governmental sphere. It emphasized a tradition running deep in American life—a tradition which was founded on the Constitutional doctrine of "life, liberty, and the pursuit of happiness" and which flourished in an economy of small landholders and individual businessmen.

There is a second tradition, equally deep-rooted in America, though perhaps less often proclaimed. This is what might be called the tradition of concern for the community which is a fundamental part of the Judaeo-Christian ethic. Curiously, some of its finest pronouncements have been made by those who are hailed as patron saints of the "free enterprise" school. Adam Smith himself, in an earlier book, "Theory of Moral Sentiments," which he is said to have regarded as finer than the "Wealth of Nations," expressed the view that "the wise and virtuous man is at all times willing that his own private interest should be sacrificed to the public interest of his own particular order or society. He is at all times willing, too, that the interest of his order or society should be sacrificed to the greater interest of the state or sovereignty of which it is only a subordinate part. He should, therefore, be equally willing that all those inferior interests should be sacrificed to the greater interest of the universe, to the interest of that great society of all sensible and intelligent beings, of which God himself is the immediate administrator and director."

Abraham Lincoln strongly emphasized the role of government in seeking this community good when he declared: "The legitimate object of government is to do for the people what needs to be done but which they cannot by individual effort do at all *or do so well for themselves.*"

It is the American businessman, paradoxically, who has been most aware of this government response to the felt needs of its people. It was they, we should remember, who sought and got from the government the huge grants of public land to help them build their railroads across the American continent. The corporation, the foundation stone of modern business, is a creation of the government; its rights and privileges are defined by law—law of Congress and the various state legislatures, not some sort of natural law pertaining to Adam Smith. Frederick Lewis Allen, commenting on the activities of businessmen at the turn of the century, has remarked: "While the eyes of boys in Economics A were fastened upon the benignity of the law of supply and demand, the eyes of corporation lawyers and their clients were fastened upon the benignity of the New Jersey Holding-Company Act. Most of these gentlemen would have regarded an income tax, let us say, as a flat transgression by man of economic law."

The gigantic amassing of capital which permitted the growth of large-scale industrialization in this country was intimately involved with the decisions of the legislative and executive branches of government on both state and national levels. And it was the third branch of government, the judiciary, which by its decisions over the years gave to corporate business most of the Constitutional rights belonging to the individual.

A change occurred in 1933, but less a fundamental change in the relation of government to the people than a heightened response to the felt needs of the people stemming from the economic debacle of 1929. To measure the real change that had come about in America, one should compare the events of 1929 with those of 1907 when a similar panic gripped Wall Street. At the earlier time the elder J. P. Morgan brought bank presidents together in meeting after meeting, much like a captain at the helm of a storm-tossed ship. As one observer noted, the Secretary of the Treasury was hardly more than one of his minor aides. Morgan bullied from the financiers the money that was necessary to bolster the weakened banks. To restore confidence in the market, he personally authorized the purchase of the Tennessee Coal and Iron Company by the Steel Corporation. Afterward, he cleared the whole transaction with President Theodore Roosevelt and the panic was over.

This was a story of private entrepreneurship at its most daring. By comparison the efforts of the Wall Street bankers to rally the market in 1929 were pathetic. Two of the financial potentates by their activities fell into the toils of the law and one went to prison. The son of Morgan was called before a Congressional committee in Washington where he suffered the ignominy of having a circus midget plopped in his lap by a prankster.

In an open letter in the *New York Times* addressed to President-elect Franklin D. Roosevelt in December of 1933 John Maynard Keynes concluded: "You have made yourself the trustee for those in every country who seek to mend the evils of our conditions by reasoned experiment within the framework of the existing social system. If you fail, rational change will be gravely prejudiced throughout the world, leaving orthodoxy and revolution to fight it out." Roosevelt entered that "reasoned experiment" with few preconceived notions. It is ironic to recall that in the campaign of 1932 his most specific pledge for alleviating the ravages of depression had been to cut government spending even closer to the bone.

Roosevelt, at least at the outset, conceived of the New Deal as primarily a resuscitating operation for the private enterprise system. His first impulse, embodied in the National Recovery Administration, was to bring businessmen themselves together in an effort to work out their mutual problems. Indicative of the New Deal's empirical nature, it was not until 1936 that Keynes, who probably did more than any other to give academic respectability to New Deal economic thought, published his major work, "The General Theory of Employment, Interest and Money." Of course, Keynes had already made many of his policy recommendations earlier. But the full impact of his thinking was more post- than pre-natal as far as the New Deal was concerned.

What Keynes did that had such importance to the New Deal, to quote John Kenneth Galbraith, was to bring about the "intellectual repeal" of Say's Law of Markets. Jean Baptiste Say, a French disciple of Adam Smith, had

promulgated the economic theorem that the act of producing goods provided the purchasing power, neither too
much nor too little, for buying them. His doctrine went
far to remove fears of either a serious depression or violent
inflation. "For well over 100 years," writes Galbraith, "it
enjoyed the standing of an article of faith. Whether a man
accepted or rejected Say's Law was, until well into the
1930's, the test of whether he was qualified for the com-
panionship of reputable scholars or should be dismissed
as a monetary crank."

According to Say's Law, money that was not being
spent would go into saving; whereupon the interest rate,
serving the same role as the price of any other commodity
in the free market, would automatically equate saving
and investment. But Keynes pointed out—and in the aftermath of the bitter depression years he found ready lis-
teners—that the interest rate did not serve to bring about
an automatic equation of savings and investments. Instead, there could be a condition of underinvestment (or
oversaving) in an economy with a resulting shortage of
purchasing power, soon followed by a fall in production,
prices, and employment. At some point, presumably, a
balance of savings effort with investment intentions would
restore the equilibrium of the economy—but at a lower
level of output and income.

What Keynes showed was that there are no automatic
governors to restore the economy to a high level of employment. On the contrary, it might well find continuing
equilibrium in a state of severe depression and unemployment. Keynes' analysis better suited the situation men
found confronting them than did the optimistic doctrines
of Adam Smith and Jean Baptiste Say.

Insufficient investment, then, became the simplified
version of Keynesian theory which had a tremendous effect on the thinking of scholars and policy makers in the

Western world. The obvious remedy, to those who were urgently concerned with remedies, was to bring about more investment. Since public funds are immediately subject to central determination by government, as private funds are not, the Keynesian remedy justified public expenditure as a way to a full employment economy. High public spending and low taxes—in short an unbalanced budget—were the weapons with which to attack underemployment. No need to worry about accumulating a public debt; in periods of full employment with inflationary tendencies the Keynesian remedy would be to switch to high taxes and low public spending, thus causing a budget surplus! Comforted by such a doctrine, government planners could face the very real welfare problems of the nation without financial anxieties.

Keynes in his wildest dreams could not have envisaged the impact which government spending in World War II would have on the American economy, pushing the employment totals of American manpower (and woman power) to fantastic heights, and bringing a growth of productivity sufficient to meet both military and essential civilian needs. But it also brought complications unforeseen by Keynesian analysis. It left the country with a national debt of some $277 billion, together with a pent-up inflationary potential resulting from the consumer restrictions of the wartime period. Present also was the continuing memory of a depression economy and the fear that the inflated postwar economy might soon turn in a steep downward direction.

Proper Keynesian analysis dictated that in such a postwar period of high level employment and inflation government should go easy on spending and hard on taxes, to create if possible a budget surplus. But, as noted in the previous chapter, the government found it difficult to exercise such rugged self-discipline in times of prosperity, more especially when a depression psychosis was present. Governmental programs once started could not be so easily switched on and off like tap water. Further, there was the added high cost of a foreign aid program made necessary by wartime destruction and the rising Communist menace. When that menace became an open military threat, the need for a multi-million-dollar armament program pretty well threw Keynesian analysis out the window. That government had grown big and showed scant prospects of getting smaller, there was little argument. But to the argument that big government had gone far toward destroying the private enterprise system, statistics from respected authorities seemed to prove the contrary. In a study sponsored by the Brookings Institution, economists A. D. H. Kaplan and Alfred E. Kahn made one remarkable discovery: "Though there have been substantial changes in the relative contributions of some of their components to national income—notably the decline in agriculture, the rise of manufacturing and of direct government operations—the available data show a remarkable balance between the larger sectors. The unregulated private production areas accounted for slightly over eighty-one per cent of economic activity in 1900; slightly under eighty per cent in 1949." Kaplan and Kahn listed among their most significant findings: the continuing expansion in the number of business enterprises; the expansion of opportunities for independent entrepreneural activity outside of agriculture; and the relative stability of the share of national income contributed by the private entrepreneur. Here was a diagnosis to soothe the fears of the most tormented businessman.

Even the argument that big government meant of necessity the fixing of a gigantic welfare system on the country has been strongly disputed by statistics cited by one economist in 1951: "In 1950 the richest nation of the world spent less than 5c of each federal tax dollar for public assistance for widows, orphans, the aged, and the blind, to help educate the nation's youth, rehabilitate the handicapped, eradicate slums, erect low-rent public housing, improve the people's health, meet the cost of all national parks, museums and libraries, and support the national school lunch program. . . . To pay for them Uncle Sam collected less than 1% of the national income in fiscal 1950. For the nation as a whole, our use of public funds, local, state, and federal—for health, education, and assistance to the needy—amounts to ⅔ of our spending on liquor and tobacco."

To all of this, the businessman critic might reply that partisans of the previous administration, no matter how much they might cling to Keynesian analysis, had contradicted the essentials of that analysis. In a time of over-investment they had proved incapable of taking the self-corrective measures which they knew to be necessary. Waste, mismanagement, and outright corruption came to substitute for genuine concern for the public welfare. They could only demand ever bigger government and further harassment of the private enterprise system. And the public ordered a halt to this by electing a new administration which could promise, in the words of Secretary of Commerce Sinclair Weeks, "to slam on the brakes and move forward in a different direction."

What we are witnessing is a fascinating and at the same time perilous experiment undertaken by men who are direct inheritors of the philosophy which holds that the harmonious working of natural law as it applies to the incentive of self-interest will result inevitably in the greatest good for the greatest number. On the outcome of this experiment, without exaggeration, depends in large part the nature of the world in which we shall live in the future. Yet, in assessing this experiment, it would not be amiss to examine some of the continuing problems that present themselves to government for solution and which may modify philosophies no matter how earnestly held.

1. *The Ever-Normal Arsenal*

For as long as the present state of world tension continues, the necessity for large-scale defense spending will continue. Though there may be differences between the so-called economy and preparedness blocs, in the main they are marginal, involving a few billion dollars out of what will remain a multi-billion dollar budget. This fact alone creates conditions having a tremendous impact on the private enterprise system. As John Knox Jessup has remarked, "The most important *single* factor in the economy is now the federal budget. And when it comes to redistributing income, neither labor unions nor the farm bloc nor any other pressure group is half as potent as the progressive income tax."

More than simply the income tax, however, the whole field of taxation to meet large government spending serves to thrust the long arm of government into the very heart of the business community. The Treasury Department and the taxation Committees of Congress by their decisions determine which businesses shall and which shall not receive special dispensations. Tax policy can measurably increase the tendency toward economic concentration, or conversely it can serve to encourage small business enterprise in the nation. Tax policy can decide among the industries which ones shall have a greater degree of liquid capital and which shall not. By the oil depletion allowance, for example, Congress has granted to the oil producer special tax concessions not available to the shoe manufacturer. This may be wise policy; but it is also governmental decision-making affecting fundamentally the operation of private enterprise.

Uncle Sam as number one customer in the nation also forcefully extends this same long arm into the economy. In the first three years after the outbreak of fighting in Korea, the government spent over 158 billion dollars for military procurement and construction. As with uranium ore purchases mentioned earlier, the normal function of price in a competitive economy means little to a market in which the government buys the total or the vast preponderance of certain commodities. Moreover, government as a continuing big purchaser can permanently change the structure of the economy. How to keep from causing the big to grow bigger and the little to be neglected, for example, is a pressing problem of defense spending. During the war years 1940-1944, the thirty-three largest corporations received over fifty percent of the prime contracts awarded; the one hundred largest got approximately two-thirds of the total. Even in subcontracting, the figures reveal that more than three-fourths of the value of those subcontracts went to firms classified as big business. According to one estimate of post-Korean military spending made in 1952 "big business" was getting approximately eighty per cent of all defense contracts.

This, in a statistical nutshell, reveals a major dilemma of defense spending affecting the private enterprise system. There are other related problems. For military reasons, government has become a major financer of industrial research; it has likewise, in its effort to boost industrial capacity, felt obliged to grant rapid tax amortization to certain businesses. Each of these activities involves enormous discretionary powers vitally affecting the private enterprise system in America. Yet few of those

who most stoutly defend the laissez-faire economy would
contend that they should be scrapped.

II. *The Do-or-Die Aspects of Welfare*

Statistics can show with reasonable preciseness the impact of defense on the industries of the nation. It is more
difficult to assess its impact elsewhere. We know that the
grouping and regrouping of population around defense
industries create vast new needs for community services,
hospitals, schools, and all the other aspects of communal
life. In a strict sense, these fall into the so-called "welfare"
activities which a business-oriented national administration of an earlier era would have regarded as out of its
bailiwick. But there are few modern businessmen who
would be inclined to overlook these needs which are intimately related to continued high productivity.

Then, there are other, longer-range "welfare" problems which will be of grave concern to government, no
matter what administration is in power. In "American
Income and Its Use," cited earlier, Joseph L. McConnell
and Janet M. Hooks delve into the fundamental problem
posed by the breakdown of the family unit in modern
American society. This is as much an economic problem as
a social one. As any businessman knows, though it is the
individual worker who counts in the production side of
the economy, it is the family which counts as the consumer
unit.

In brief, according to the authors' analysis, both the
clan-family of primitive society and the *stem*-family of a
primarily agricultural society (in which the elder married
child maintains the family farm while the others go into
commerce and industry) provided a fairly good social

security system. There was always the old homestead to return to in time of need. But with modern industrial and
primarily urban society there has arisen what sociologists
call the *conjugal*-family which preserves the close parent-
child relationship only to the point of the child's marriage.

Despite the benefits coming with it—higher average income and greater freedom for the individual—the con-
jugal-family has had its price. A part of that price is the
dependency problem of wife and children in the family
broken by divorce, separation, or death. Another part is
the problem of the aged, cast adrift from family ties, who
are faced with the need of support during years length-
ened by the very technology of modern society. It is startling to realize the rapid growth of that segment of our
population past the age of 65; it should be even more
startling to those who must concern themselves with the
economic problems of America to learn that an estimated
five-sixths of those aged will have no private provision for
self-support.

Thus the problem of poverty in America takes on new
dimensions. There can no longer be the callous indifference of an earlier age when the social security of the large
family unit could be presumed to take care of those un-
fortunates who have no means of earning a living income.
As for the notion that the aged should have made adequate provision for their own support, there is eloquent
answer in the simple statistic that two lifetime annuities of
$75 per month for a couple past sixty-five cost $25,000.
There are very few income earners in America who have
been able to accumulate such a sum. And so far, as the
authors point out, Federal Old Age and Survivors Insurance has proven woefully inadequate.

The problem of poverty becomes all the more relevant
in an economy which, uniquely in world history, must
concern itself with the distribution of abundance, not
scarcity. Most businessmen and economists alike, while

by no means resolved on many important questions related to income distribution in a high productivity economy, recognize the simple fact that unattended poverty can have an economically dampening effect on the whole. John Donne's adage—"ask not for whom the bell tolls"—has sound economic foundations.

Margaret G. Reid, Professor of Economics at the University of Chicago, in "American Income and Its Use," has made a statistical analysis of the distribution of income in this country. She finds, interestingly, that income distribution has been slowly moving toward equality among economic groups in the last two decades. This has been true for geographical sections of the country, with the steady rise of the underdeveloped regions like the South; for functional groups, in which the farmer's improvement over the past two decades deserves notice; and for racial minorities, the Negro especially. Professor Reid points out, however, that this movement does not necessarily indicate greater equality within a particular group. She finds, for example, that despite remedial farm legislation, the small farmer has not profited to nearly the same degree as the large farmer.

One factor in this movement toward equalization, as Professor Reid indicates, has been action by the government, particularly progressive taxation. But another factor possibly even more meaningful has been the tremendous rise in productivity in this country. Professor Reid cautions that the requirements of a dynamic economy can be quite distinct from those of a static one. Whereas in a static economy there might be unreserved rejoicing over any measures that tend toward equalization of income distribution, in a dynamic economy the drive for ever-increasing productivity makes desirable an accumulation of wealth among producer groups.

All these problems falling broadly in the "welfare"—or more properly speaking "general welfare"—category, will continue to present themselves urgently for consideration to government, no matter what administration may be in power. Surely, only the most narrow-minded citizen can fail to grasp the interlocking responsibility of government and private enterprise in meeting them.

III.   Self-Interest versus the General Good

Finally, there are problems of government which are not new, but which have a particular relevancy for government today. Even the ardent believer in free enterprise cannot ignore the fact, as any Secretary of Agriculture will attest, that certain sectors of the economy differ markedly from others. Agriculture, without price supports and occasional crop quotas, would be a highly competitive, free enterprise system in the best classical sense. But the farmer must buy the things he needs in a market where oligopolistic business practices a more restrained brand of competition with very little price fluctuation. As experience has abundantly proved, he usually comes off second best in such a situation, and not merely in a depression economy. After the brief post-World War I boom, farm prices began a steady drop over the decade of the 'twenties while the industrial price index moved equally steadily upward. Since 1951, again, farm prices have been dropping. Yet, as in the case of petroleum products, the things the farmer has to buy continued to rise in price, often quite arbitrarily. Because he constitutes an important numerical— and therefore political—element of the population, government cannot fail to respond to this problem with all the techniques at its disposal.

Of course, there is a wide spectrum of regulatory activity in which even the most anti-government spokesmen would probably agree that government has a role to play.

The Interstate Commerce, the Federal Trade and the Federal Power Commissions are among the regulatory commissions which have found a degree of acceptance even by those they regulate. Too often overlooked, however, is the disturbing fact that the regulated often appear to be regulating the regulator.

Government cannot abdicate its responsibility by failing to measure the public interest against the special interest demands made on it, frequently by those who clamor loudest for the "free enterprise" way. We mentioned earlier, for example, Assistant Interior Secretary Wormser who speaks of freeing the mining industry from its fetters. Yet he was formerly head of the Lead and Zinc Trade Association which has lobbied for what would amount to a parity price on domestic lead and zinc. He has openly supported such provisions in the Simpson Bill which truly brings his attitude toward government round full circle. He has colleagues in this seeming ambivalence. The small retail druggist, for example, demands effective government intervention to prevent monopolistic practices of the chains, yet he fights for Fair Trade legislation to permit uniform pricing for the products he sells.

These are tensions that may be expected to continue so long as we have a "mixed" economy in which the tradition of freedom and the tradition of social responsibility are kept in healthy balance. They will not be automatically resolved by permitting government to take over everything, nor, alternatively, by seeking to free the economic system from all involvement with government. As Professor Niebuhr has said, "Dogmatic presuppositions, whether laissez-faire dogmatics, or socialistic dogmatics, make for injustice, and the best societies have a mixture of strategies which seek to guarantee freedom on the one hand and justice on the other hand."

In "Goals of Economic Life," Robert Morrison Mac-Iver, Professor Emeritus at Columbia University, and

Frank H. Knight, Professor of Social Sciences and Philosophy at the University of Chicago, examine this relationship between the political and the economic systems. They emphasize that both should be regarded as "two great means-structures" to be used by the citizen in pursuit of his goals, neither to be regarded as a goal in itself. Each is a power system, and to the extent that its power goes unchecked it represents a danger to the individual. The great hope for the individual is to strike a balance between the two—a sort of equilibrium in which one power serves to restrain the other, thereby permitting the individual maximum freedom and maximum justice.

Professor MacIver concludes: "A free society is a flexible society, always experimenting, always, so far as it is also intelligent, seeking to adjust its conditions to its changing needs. It enthrones no dogma, it surrenders to no power system. Whatever mistakes it makes it never binds its own future." With such a dynamic concept Adam Smith, were he alive today instead of embalmed in the legend of his disciples, would undoubtedly agree.

CHAPTER VIII

The Church and the Kingdom

ONE CANNOT FIX a precise year, but by the latter part of
the nineteenth century the revolution in values had come
full round. From the Middle-Age ecclesiastical outlook in
which the whole process of getting and spending was
tolerated as a necessary concession to human frailty in a
material world, it had come to the point where the church
(or at least the Protestant church) was considered as
scarcely more than a ceremonial ratification of the morality that prevailed.

The story of this era has been told brilliantly by Henry
F. May in "Protestant Churches and Industrial America."
According to May, there was a low water mark of some sort
in the year 1877. In July of that year a sudden ten per cent
wage cut on most of the railroads east of the Mississippi
precipitated the most destructive labor battle in American
history. Trains were halted; troops fought with angry
mobs; bloodshed and fire mounted in Baltimore, Pittsburgh, and other railroad centers. It was the first genuine
shock to expanding industrialism—a shock for which the
church was no more prepared than the businessman. The
well-known Congregationalist minister, Henry Ward
Beecher, whose large salary and still more handsome

royalties in newspaper revenue enabled him to indulge fairly extravagant tastes for driving fine horses and carrying pocketfuls of uncut gems, denounced the railroad employees in strident tones for not being willing to bear their poverty more nobly:

> "It is said that a dollar a day is not enough for a wife and five or six children. No, not if the man smokes or drinks beer. It is not enough if they are to live as he would be glad to have them live. It is not enough to enable them to live as perhaps they would have a right to live in prosperous times. But is not a dollar a day enough to buy bread with? Water costs nothing; and a man who cannot live on bread is not fit to live. What is the use of a civilization that simply makes men incompetent to live under the conditions which exist . . ."

The so-called neo-Calvinism of the Gilded Age was voiced by a number of eloquent divines. The Reverend Russell Conwell's popular sermon, "Acres of Diamonds," delivered according to his own estimate six thousand times with a total earning of $8,000,000, expressed all too well the acclimatization of Christianity to capitalist America. "To secure wealth is an honorable ambition, and is one great test of a person's usefulness to others . . . I say, get rich, get rich!" For Conwell, success was linked to morality: ". . . 98 out of 100 of the rich men of America are honest. That is why they are rich." And conversely poverty was something depraved. "I won't give in but what I sympathize with the poor," said Conwell, "but the number of poor who are to be sympathized with is very small. To sympathize with a man whom God has punished for his sins, thus to help him when God would still continue a just punishment, is to do wrong, no doubt about it . . ."

For Conwell, a businessman turned preacher, this emphasis on material things was not entirely unexpected. But the continuing great popularity of his lecture and others like it demonstrated that a great many American Christians believed that the old virtue of self-help was a sufficient solution to social problems and was sanctioned by Christian morality. As Bishop William Lawrence of Massachusetts stated flatly, "Godliness is in league with riches. . . . Material prosperity is helping to make the national character sweeter, more joyous, more unselfish, more Christlike." Whereas for Cotton Mather a man's worldly calling had been one of the two oars (the other being spiritual) by which he could propel his boat to the "shoar of eternal blessedness," Bishop Lawrence, as one observer remarked, had transformed Mather's rowboat into an ocean liner.

For such a creed even charity as a Christian virtue was to be cultivated more for improvement to self than for good done to others. The Reverend Horace Bushnell, for instance, preaching on the duties proper to the high calling of the merchant, cautioned the Christian in commerce that he must carry on his business strictly according to the laws of trade "and never let his operations be mixed up with charities . . ." As an example of the type of benevolence that would be most fitting, Bushnell suggested that the merchant set aside "remnants, faded and smirched, and smoked, and shelf-worn goods, and styles of goods gone by . . . all which he would otherwise put in auction and sell at great loss to himself." These carefully selected materials, Bushnell said in a sermon published in 1873, should be sold to the poor at low prices.

The ethics of orthodoxy had become, in the words of one writer, "a sterile union of individualism and formalism," a staunch defender of the *status quo,* going out of its way to criticize economic or political change. "The advocates of spiritualism, of woman's rights, of social changes of nearly every kind, have nearly all of them been touched with a liberalism amounting to Deism, and are inclined to reject as authoritative the Old and New Testament writers," declared the editor of the *Biblical Reportory and Princeton Review* in 1868. Yet, that editor expressed a firm conviction that Christianity would be able to work out the "true solution of the problems of this world . . ." It would do this "through the power of God in Jesus Christ to develop and ennoble the whole character of man." Ironically, this same tradition in the Christian church, eschewing each new social program over the past century as opposite to God's intention, was to come heartily to the support of the sweeping twentieth-century social reform known as "Prohibition."

But a counter-revolution was already in the making. "In 1876," writes May, "Protestantism presented a massive, almost unbroken front in its defense of the social status quo. Two decades later social criticism had penetrated deeply into each major church. Some of the most prominent Protestant leaders were calling for social reform; Christian radicals, not unheard, were demanding complete reorganization of society. . . . The immediate cause of this important change lay neither in theological innovation nor in the world climate of opinion, but in the resistless intrusion of social crisis, and particularly in a series of large-scale, violent labor conflicts."

There were three major periods of labor strife. In 1877, the railroad strikes mentioned above; in 1886, a nation-wide series of strikes culminating in the disastrous bomb explosion in Chicago's Haymarket; and in 1892-94, a new series starting with the attempted wage reduction at the Carnegie Steel Corporation. In the heat of these violently emotional episodes, church editorial opinion seemed no less violent than that of the industrial leaders who were being challenged. *The Congregationalist*, for example, a leading church publication, could remark in 1877:

"Bring on then the troops—the armed police—in
overwhelming numbers. Bring out the Gatling guns.
Let there be no fooling with blank cartridges. But
let the mob know, everywhere, that for it to stand
one moment after it has been ordered by proper authorities to disperse, will be to be shot down in its
tracks. . . . A little of the vigor of the first Napoleon
is the thing we now need."

In 1892, the *Christian Advocate* was shocked by the
theory that a company had an obligation to confer with
its employees: "Extend the rights of the state to the com-
pelling of men or corporations to confer with representatives of labor, and you have despotism or Bellamyism
forthwith . . ."

Yet, shocked out of their complacency, the Christian
ministers in the aftermath of the great strike waves com-
menced a search for solutions to the new problems. More
and more came to realize that the all-sufficient optimistic
formulas expounded by men like Henry Ward Beecher
had been shattered by unanswerable events. More and
more Protestant leaders began to voice the kind of criticism of the existing order which has been broadly characterized as the Social Gospel.

Exponents of the Social Gospel did not bring some new
religion to America, though many of their critics at the
time would have so claimed. The theologian Richard Niebuhr, in his "The Kingdom of God in America," effectively disputes the idea that Protestantism has consisted
of a series of antithetical developments throughout its
history in this country. He compares it rather to a "sym-
phony in which each movement has its own specific
theme, yet builds on all that has gone before and com-
bines with what follows so that the meaning of the whole
can be apprehended only as the whole is heard."

So it was that the church leaders, faced by the great

problems confronting them in industrially expanding America, found in their religion the sanctions for a growing social consciousness. There were men like Washington Gladden, who has been called Father of the Social Gospel. In 1876 Gladden's ideas were about the same as those of many others who looked at the social unrest with fear and horror. His book entitled "Working People and Their Employers" published about that time, expressed views based on a profoundly classical economic theory. In times of depression, he said, laborers should take any work they are offered, no matter how ill paid, and some should return to the farm. He implied that a more cooperative form of society might someday replace the wage system, but to reach this goal he prescribed only the usual formula: that workingmen should save and buy shares in industry.

But in 1882 Gladden was called to the pastorate of the First Congregational Church of Columbus, Ohio, where he soon found himself involved on a personal basis with a great labor struggle, the Hocking Valley coal strike of 1884. Several of the principal officers of the coal company were members of Gladden's congregation and he knew that they were determined to break the union. They succeeded at the time, but a year later the strike broke out again and ended this time with success for the miners.

This experience in trade unionism stirred Gladden deeply. From then on his utterances on labor, often delivered to audiences of employers, showed a personal intimate understanding of labor's problems. He was strongly opposed to socialism which was attracting a number of intellectuals at the time, but he reserved his greatest wrath for unbending conservatives and particularly for the theory that wages were meant to be determined by competitive forces. "The labor of the nation is the life of the nation," he declared. "Is that a commodity to be bought in the cheapest market and sold in the dearest?

. . . The Christian moralist is, therefore, bound to admonish the Christian employer that the wage-system, when it rests on competition as its sole basis, is antisocial and anti-Christian." Gladden looked with a scholar's purpose into the facts of the workingman's share of the wealth of the expanding economy. His startling conclusion was that labor had tripled its production in twenty-five years without materially increasing its receipts. In a stirring address to an audience mostly composed of striking employees in Cleveland, Gladden described the situation as one of war. "If war is the order of the day," he concluded, "we must grant labor belligerent rights."

Despite such strong sentiments, Gladden possessed a temperate manner and personal charm which won him wide approval among his audiences, even those who disagreed strongly with his views. In the main, his preachments about the fatherhood of God and the brotherhood of man were understandable and frequently acceptable to the untheoretical, worldly, optimistic congregations of his time. Gladden, unlike some of his contemporaries, never ventured into sheer humanism; he kept contact with the powerful Christian tradition in which he and his hearers had been nurtured.

Such was not the fate of all the members of the Social Gospel movement. There was, for example, the controversial and prominent Christian Radical, George E. Herron, who blazed across the nation during the 'nineties with his own concept of Social Christianity. Speaking first as a Congregational Minister in Burlington, Iowa, and later as a professor of applied Christianity at Iowa College (holding a chair established for him by a devoted follower), Herron drew wild enthusiasm and equally wild opposition wherever he went. Before his influence in church circles came to an abrupt end in 1901 (when he was divorced and quickly remarried under questionable circumstances), his widespread preaching of the Social

Gospel had evolved steadily in the direction of pure socialism without too much Christian content. Yet his influence among many of the church people throughout the country was tremendous. He was partly responsible for the founding of the American Institute of Christian Sociology at Chautauqua. Inspired partly by Herron, partly by a curious mixture of ideas drawn from Karl Marx, St. Francis, and Jesus, by way of Leo Tolstoi, there gathered on a thousand-acre plot in Georgia in 1895 the "Christian Commonwealth Colony," a community of 300 to 400 people who for the next four years conducted one of those recurring but unsuccessful experiments in pure utopian communism.

If Gladden was the "Father" of the Social Gospel, Walter Rauschenbusch has been well designated its "Prophet." His pre-eminence rested as much upon his unique personality as upon the force of his ideas. He was deeply and sincerely religious, but had none of the fanaticism of Herron. He was not as practical as Gladden but had even more popular appeal. His book "Christianity and the Social Crisis," published in 1907, established him at once as the recognized leader of the Social Gospel.

It was Rauschenbusch who emphasized the central concept of the Kingdom of God which he believed to have been the heart of Jesus' teaching. He based both his criticism of modern society and his program for its reformation on his belief in an Immanent, Active God. Through God's indwelling in men there could be predicated a human society whose progressive perfection would attain the divine kingdom of righteousness and justice. For Rauschenbusch the Protestant Reformation had failed to place this Kingdom hope in its proper context. Instead the church had grown up as the center of Christian attention. Deprived of the mighty social mission which he felt that Christ had brought, theology had lost its inspiration. "The Kingdom of God breeds prophets; the church breeds priests and theologians," he wrote. And it was to promote this Kingdom on earth that he devoted his tremendous inspirational efforts.

Rauschenbusch's Christian socialism sounded at times like pure socialism with a religious content added; at other times it had more vague foundations. For him the "saved" institutions in society—the family, education, church, cooperatives—are the democratic ones, whereas the "unsaved" ones—corporations, monopolies, war—are autocratic. The job of social man is to bring about the repentance and conversion of professions and organizations. This could be accomplished by having them give up monopoly power and income derived from legalized extortion and come under the law of service, content with a fair income for honest work. Genuine democracy was Rauschenbusch's abiding goal; whether it took the form of pure socialism or not, he appeared not altogether certain.

These were the outstanding and controversial leaders of the Social Gospel movement. The ranks included many others holding a variety of specific social aims but embracing in common an awakened social consciousness and claiming theological foundations for it in Christ's teachings. From the vantage point of the mid-twentieth century some of their preachments sound utopian and naive in the extreme. But the effect of their moral fervor was profound at the time. William Allen White, the noted newspaper editor, has described his own departure from straight plutocratic politics in these terms:

". . . it was not until the turn of the century that I began to understand the New Testament.

"I have no recollection that I ever traveled on the road to Damascus. But Theodore Roosevelt and his attitude toward the powers that be, the status quo, the economic, social and political order, certainly did begin to penetrate my heart. And when I came to the New Testament and saw Jesus, not as a figure in theology—the only begotten son who saved by his blood a sinful world—but as a statesman and philosopher who dramatized his creed by giving his life for it, then gradually the underpinning of my Pharisaic philosophy was knocked out. Slowly as the new century came into its first decade, I saw the Great Light. Around me in that day scores of young leaders in American politics and public affairs were seeing what I saw, feeling what I felt."

Social Gospel leaders found new revelations in Christ's social teachings. Even the top political leaders glimpsed something of that Great Light. Theodore Roosevelt was directly in contact with several Social Gospel leaders, including Rauschenbusch. He not only endorsed but promoted the Social Gospel. "The Church must fit itself for the practical betterment of mankind if it is to attract and retain the fealty of the men best worth holding and using," he said. "Under the tense activity of modern social and industrial conditions the Church, if it is to give real leadership, must grapple, zealously, fearlessly, and cool-headedly with the problems of social and industrial justice."

Woodrow Wilson's sudden switch toward Social Christianity paralleled his political turn toward progressivism. In 1909 he had specifically opposed the Social Gospel:

"For my part, I do not see any promise of vitality either in the Church or in society except upon the true basis of individualism . . . He (the minister) must preach Christianity to men, not to society. He must preach salvation to the individual, for it is only one by one that we can love, and love is the law of life."

By 1914, however, Wilson had completely changed his mind:

> "For one I am not fond of thinking of Christianity as the means of saving *individual* souls . . . Christ came into the world to save others, not to save himself, and no man is a true Christian who does not think constantly of how he can lift his brother, how he can enlighten mankind, how he can make virtue the rule of conduct in the circle in which he lives."

Later Protestants have been severely critical of some of the excesses of the Social Gospel movement. They claim that it constantly tended to lose its theological footing despite the sturdiness of such leaders as Gladden and Rauschenbusch. In reinterpreting the major Christian beliefs in terms of an Immanent God working not only through man but through society, atonement seemed to become little more than a symbol of suffering for the good of others, sin was selfishness overcome by education, and the Kingdom of God was merely the working out of the Divine Will through gradual social improvement.

Perhaps an even more telling weakness was its transcendent optimism. John Wright Buckham has admitted that "it seemed to many of us who were studying theology and beginning our ministry in the 'eighties and 'nineties as if humanity were on the eve of the golden age. . . . The Kingdom of God appeared to be at hand. . . . As the dawn of the twentieth century approached we felt sure that it meant the ushering in of the reign of universal brotherhood." Another minister, Josiah Strong, could declare during those optimistic 'nineties:

> ". . . such is my confidence in the saving power of the complete Gospel, that in my very soul I believe

a single generation will suffice to solve the problem of pauperism, to wipe out the saloon, to inaugurate a thousand needed reforms, and really change the face of society, provided only the churches generally enter into this movement."

Such optimism may have sufficed during an age given over to optimism. But when the Social Gospel ran into the deeper "jungles and morasses" of the twentieth century, its simple social analysis could not make the grade. Its shallow theological underpinnings proved insufficient spiritual sustenance to a great many Americans at a time when recurring crises were the order of the day.

Badly wrecked by the first World War, the Social Gospel dwindled as a clearly identifiable movement within the Protestant Church and gradually split asunder during the postwar era. In the 'thirties a new theological movement gained headway which for some has supplanted the Social Gospel with a "deeper" theology which can have meaning to the individual living in a tragic era. Yet for the most part there has also been an intense effort to preserve the practical, ethical idealism inherited from the Social Gospel tradition.

John C. Bennett, in his little volume "Christian Ethics and Social Policy" describes three major characteristics that have carried over from the Social Gospel heritage to play a large part in the social movement today in most churches. The first is the great emphasis on Christian social responsibility. There is no blinking at the knowledge we now have of the extent to which a person is conditioned by society. Nowadays few would try to claim that the soul is a completely independent entity having its own freedom apart from body and environment. The Christian can feel genuine concern for the spiritual effects of bad housing, slum conditions, and unemployment which have, in the words of Archbishop Temple, "power to corrupt any man not already far advanced in saintliness."

A second characteristic, according to Bennett, is the acceptance of the fact that radical change in the structure of society is to be expected and that we cannot simply believe that what *exists* must be ordained by God. The church has been freed from uncritical support of the social hierarchy in many lands. Finally, a third characteristic is the tendency of Christians to try to see the world from the point of view of the classes and races that have been most oppressed or neglected in the past.

Withal, there is a new awareness, pretty much lacking in the old Social Gospel, of the stubbornness of evil in the world and the depth and persistence of sin in our life. Without such awareness, the Christian would despair before the Communist atrocities in Korea, and even the bigotry and hatred in our own country. With this awareness, he has sought deeper spiritual insight into the nature of man and the meaning of Christ's teachings. A highly significant part of this search lies in that body of thought known as "Christian realism" of which Reinhold Niebuhr is probably the best-known American exponent. Niebuhr has maintained that the Social Gospel's emphasis upon love as a sufficient resource in resolving the conflicts inherent in society is unrealistic and even naive. It ignores the strength of self-interest and pride in the heart of man. In other words, classical Christianity was right in its emphasis on original sin. There must be no false expectations about building the Kingdom of God within history. There is the firm belief, however, that though God's kingdom transcends every social achievement, we do serve God in each endeavor to raise the level of human life, in every new embodiment of justice and mercy and fellowship in our communities. While there is no such thing as a Christian economic system, there are immediate Christian goals for economic life.

One important part of our modern Christian heritage are the institutions which grew up as a result of the Social Gospel. In 1908 thirty denominations came together in Philadelphia to establish the Federal Council of Churches. From the outset, with its Commission on the Church and Social Service, the Federal Council displayed a strong sense of social responsibility, fighting *against* the seven-day work week, child labor, unhealthy working conditions for women; fighting *for* healthy industrial conditions, old age insurance, the right of employees to organize, and a living minimum wage.

It is not possible here to trace in detail the evolution from the Federal Council's inception until today. Undoubtedly it and the other interdenominational councils which grew up in the years following have been in the main stream of American Protestant thought. In 1950 when twelve interdenominational agencies came together to form the National Council of Churches, the Christian unity movement had reached a peak. By 1953 the National Council included a fellowship of thirty nationwide churches with more than thirty-four million members. Practically every major historical body of American Christianity except the Roman Catholic was united in this movement. In turn, this fellowship has been still further widened in the World Council of Churches, formed in 1948.

The National Council of Churches does not presume to lay down doctrinal formulations, nor for that matter to take definitive stands on specific social issues. But in studying its work one can assess the direction of Protestant thought. The declaration of faith in Jesus Christ as Divine Lord and Savior, embedded in the Constitution of the National Council, has been kept in its primal place in Christian belief. The Social Gospel is being grounded in a deeper theology. The social conscience of the Church, awakened by the pioneers of the Social Gospel in the late nineteenth century, has not returned to slumber. Under the dynamic leadership of the National Council's Department on the Church and Economic Life the quest for a Christian approach to the major economic problems of our time continues. Church leaders have shed the easy optimism of the early Social Gospel and re-examined some of the fundamental precepts. Particularly, they have come to reassess the value of private enterprise economy as an independent power system giving balance to the political and permitting the individual best to exercise his freedom. There is no tendency toward an easy acceptance of complete laissez faire or complete socialism.

On the other hand, there is no tendency to abdicate Christian responsibility. As the General Assembly of the National Council declared in a message adopted at its meeting in Denver, Colorado, December 1952:

"All Christian Churches . . . have a prophetic role to play within the national life. It is their duty so to sensitize the conscience of the nation and of all classes and institutions within it that no group of citizens shall arrogate to itself perpetual rights and privileges which it denies to others."

An important part of the National Council's job has been the work of reconciliation—pulling together Christian laymen from various walks of life in a mutual effort to work out satisfactory agreements of ways to meet their pressing problems. Such was the North American Lay Conference on "The Christian and His Daily Work" held in Buffalo, New York, in February 1952. There the laymen broke up into occupational groups, attorneys, farm operators, industrial management, insurance, labor leaders, etc., each seeking to discover a Christian approach to the specific problems confronting its members in their daily life.

There is the firmest conviction that Christian insights are relevant to the present age, and with this conviction comes a determination to examine the great concepts of our national life—"democracy," "freedom," and "security." In a publication, "The National Council of Churches Views Its Task in Christian Life and Work," published in May of 1951, a serious attempt is made to articulate this sense of responsibility the Christian feels which goes deeper than his belief in any existing economic system or particular way of life. The Christian views the threat of Communism as a greater threat than simply a challenge to private property. He endorses particular aspects of the economic system as developed in America without committing himself or his Christianity to a blanket endorsement of the whole. He is goaded in his search by that "divine discontent" which is ever mindful of the need for both freedom and justice. He is eternally belligerent against the evil effects of poverty both within our borders and in other lands. He seeks that balance of flexibility and stability in economic life which will provide for individual and group security within a dynamic economy.

Christians in America make no claims to unity on a specific set of political or economic programs. But there is nonetheless the persistent attempt in church life to bridge the barriers, to break down the irreconcilables, so that economic or political concepts will not be allowed to harden into unmalleable support for or opposition to the *status quo*. A persistent study of Christ's social teachings serves as guide and moderator in this mission.

There is no turning back in principle to the former individualism in the theological or ecclesiastical leadership of the churches. Take one illustration. The World

Council of Churches is now organizing the Second World Assembly in Evanston, Illinois, in 1954. Six Commissions are preparing for the discussion at the Assembly, dealing with such vital subjects as international affairs, intergroup relations (mostly race), social and economic problems under the heading "The Responsible Society," work in modern society in the context of Christian vocation, evangelism, and church union. Four of these subjects have a direct connection with the Christianity of social consciousness. In approaching them, many church leaders in America feel a special responsibility to emphasize those aspects of the capitalist system which make for a healthy Christian environment, the more so because Christian leaders in Europe and Asia are widely committed to a radical criticism of capitalism. Yet they feel that it is equally important not to have an American "capitalist" bloc in the World Council with a special political and economic axe to grind, nor to appear to argue that there can be no such thing as Christian socialism.

In this churning, hopeful process of creative work somehow the balance may be righted which was so sadly overturned in the previous century. Once again Christ's message may be made meaningful to modern highly organized society. There can be no such meaning in a Christianity which clings to the old individualism of the nineteenth century and which gives unquestioned defense to the *status quo* in political and economic life.

The encouraging aspect of this search for new meaning has been its widespread and cooperative nature. But this is not to say that there has not been opposition, and indeed violent opposition. We have already mentioned the critique of the Social Gospel advanced by certain religious thinkers in America; the caution against its unbridled optimism, the need to find firmer theological foundations for the church's activities.

But there is even more serious opposition to Christian social consciousness, perhaps most eloquently expressed by James Agee:

"It is fashionable to feel, and to force upon others, an acute sense of social responsibility. . . . People have been badgered half out of their minds by the sense of a sort of global responsibility: the relentless daily obligation to stay aware of, hep to, worked-up over, guilty towards, active about, the sufferings of people at a great distance for whom one can do nothing whatever; a sort of playing-at-God (since He is in exile) over every sparrow that falls, with the sense of virtue increasing in ratio to the distance. This enormous and nonsensical burden can be dropped with best intelligence and grace by religious men; in any case by Christians. Believing in the concern, wisdom, and mercy of God and in ultimate justice, roughly aware of how much (and how little) attempts at social betterment can bring, rid of illusory responsibilities, Christians can undertake real and sufficient ones: each to do no less than he as a human being is able (and he is not apt to be a saint) for the human beings within his sight and reach and touch; and never to presume it other than anti-human to do more. Thus alone, it becomes possible to be quiet, to begin to learn a little bit thoroughly, directly, through the heart; to begin, in fact to be human." (1)

Few men have not felt at one time or another some of Agee's sentiments. He points to the real danger that the busy, busy churchman may lose all contact with reality by his entanglement in organizational paperwork, his preoccupation with humanity by remote control. Yet

1 *Partisan Review*, Feb. 1950, pp. 108-9.

because such a danger is real, one must not overlook the escapism that permeates Agee's words. Quietness is no virtue when it means consciously removing oneself from the world's sounds. The humanity Agee describes can best be found in a monastery.

But far more serious, there has been a bitter attack on the major Protestant church movements by those who seem to have other than religious motivations. When the Methodist Bishop G. Bromley Oxnam appeared before the House Un-American Activities Committee in July 1953, a phalanx of his fellow ministers was present to lend him moral support. But other ministers were there for quite different reasons. In the front row sat leading representatives of the American Council of Churches, a factional group which has repeatedly attacked Oxnam, as well as other leading churchmen. In a recent book, "Apostles of Discord," a young Methodist minister, Ralph Lord Roy, probes into this bitter strife within the Protestant churches and points to those who are provoking the most dissension. It is a fascinating book, highly valuable reading for anyone who wishes to understand some of the forces at play in the nation's church life.

As Roy points out, there have been a few in the church movement, nurtured in the Social Gospel tradition, who came to embrace the gospel of Karl Marx rather than the Gospel of Jesus Christ. The very looseness of Protestant church organization, one of its great democratic virtues, has made it impossible peremptorily to excommunicate such groups.

But the number of these extreme-left-wing Protestants has been exceedingly small; there is absolutely no evidence that they render more than occasional lip service to Moscow propaganda. To use them as the reason for launching a full-fledged attack on the clergy as do some like J. B. Matthews ("The largest single group supporting the Communist apparatus in the United States is composed of Protestant clergymen") is to render a great evil in pursuing a small one.

The campaign to promote discord is being waged at full tilt. Recently, the National Council of Churches issued a statement defending itself and its leaders against a smear attack from a small but well-financed group called the American Council of Christian Laymen. The major mission of this fanatical group has been to distribute a brochure which by false charges and innuendo seeks to prove that the Soviet Hammer and Sickle stands behind the great national church organization representing more than thirty-four million Christians.

It is difficult to understand what prompts Christians thus recklessly to challenge the loyalty of fellow Christians. Certainly politics plays a larger role than theology. One prominent Christian leader has remarked that these extremists are concentrating a reactionary attack on the Church because they know that they have lost out as far as taking over either major political party is concerned. Perhaps the most disturbing aspect is the evidence that a number of wealthy individuals and corporations have contributed financially to their vicious campaigns.

To those who enunciate these flagrant misstatements, the Christian ethic demands a dogmatic creed, as well as an absolutist economic and political philosophy. Paradoxically, Tawney, whose "Religion and the Rise of Capitalism" first traced the religio-economic patterns of Protestantism, firmly denies that there is this inherent rigidity. "In every human soul there is a socialist and an individualist, an authoritarian and a fanatic for liberty," he wrote, "as in each there is a Catholic and a Protestant. The same is true of the mass movements in which men marshal themselves for common action. There was in Puritanism an element which was conservative and traditionalist, and an element which was revolutionary; a collectivism which grasped at an iron discipline, and an individualism which spurned the savorless mess of human ordinances; a sober prudence which would garner the fruits of this world, and a divine recklessness which would make all things new."

The church must maintain a place for such diverse elements or lose all. There is room for the conservative, room for those for whom Christ's teachings have a broader social compulsion. The church's high mission for our times will be sadly frustrated if, through fratricidal warfare, it fails to help men restore the vital balance that for long has been upset.

CHAPTER IX

Technology, Creator and Destroyer

WE HAVE SEEN that a deep and continuing concern for the conduct of life from day to day has characterized Christianity virtually since the beginning of the Christian era. Deriving from the Greco-Judaeo-Christian tradition, this concern has often taken coercive and even violent form. One consequence has been a prolonged and some- times painful but not unhealthy conflict between the con- science of the individual and the authority of Church and State. The ethical and religious concern for the con- duct of daily life has provided the sanctions for a frame- work of law enclosing an orderly society. And when such sanctions, as a part of a popular and widely accepted ethos, have been weakened the effect of law has been doubtful indeed.

The faith that the greatest good derives inevitably from the free and untrammeled expression of each individual's self-interest, with religion and ethics set off in a separate and private compartment, is of recent emphasis. Further- more, even when it was most widely accepted toward the end of the nineteenth century, there were always those who maintained that self-interest was not an automatic gyroscope to keep society on an even keel; that ethics was not a rarefied department of life reserved for theoretical discussion two or three hours a week.

Yet the conviction that the good man, the preacher in the pulpit for example, should know his place and stay strictly in it took a deep hold. He was to set a convenient example of virtue apart from the hard bargaining, the harsh conflicts, the loud dissensions of the market place. If one cared to hear him on Sunday, it was comforting to know that the Christian ideal was still carefully preserved. For many, particularly in America, religion retained the apocalyptic overtones that it had in its origins and, therefore, what happened to one on earth mattered little at all since the day of judgment and the dissolution of all earthly things were close at hand.

One of the great Christians of our time who strove mightily to break down the walls erected to separate God, man and business was the late Archbishop William Temple in England. In his "Christianity and the Social Order" he relates an incident that illustrates strikingly the extent to which the divorce had come to be taken for granted. As the bitter labor dispute in the coal mines deteriorated into the general strike of 1926, a group of bishops came forward to offer their services to the government in helping to resolve what would have seemed in any other country threat of actual civil war. The then Prime Minister, Stanley Baldwin, said no thank you with considerable acerbity, adding that it would be just as logical to call on the Iron and Steel Federation to take part in the revision of the Athanasian Creed as it would be to expect the bishops to contribute anything to the easing of a great social-economic crisis.

Archbishop Temple offered in the course of his lifetime a full and vigorous prescription for remaking society on a more nearly Christian pattern. He recommended a drastic shift in the claim on production from ownership to labor. It was not that he would abolish capital or capitalism. But his formula for the "withering dividend" provided for an end of the claim of the stockholder after he had received dividends for a certain period of years equal to a certain ratio of the value of his investment. There was thus much that was naive in the Temple prescription.

But the fundamental fallacy resulted not so much from his lofty idealism as from the view that has colored so much of the Labor and Socialist thinking in Great Britain. This is a fixation on the redistribution of the available goods and services. That view simply does not take into account the element that has made American capitalism unique in the world. The element, it is hardly necessary to add, is ever greater productivity which thereby constantly tends to lower prices and makes more and more goods available to more and more people.

The economy of Great Britain and Western Europe had become tightly bound around by the development of monopolies held together by cartels. The re-distributive approach of European socialism owes not a little to this confinement. Since there seemed to be no way out, the only solution was to divide up what lay within the walls, giving to the many the share that had been held by the few. A consequence, as socialism gained in political power, was the nationalization of major industries. They had too often been stagnant for lack of competition and new drafts of capital; therefore the shift from a private and static bureaucracy to the static bureaucracy of state control was not too great a shift.

Again and again during the past hundred years we have seen conspicuous examples of how not to solve the problems of an industrial, technological society. In this category the prize exhibit is, of course, Soviet Russia. The power put into the hands of a managerial clique has been used with ever-increasing authoritarianism. In the Marxian structure no check whatsoever is put upon the exercise of power by the little group at the controls. Here is a formula for autocracy of the most ruthless sort.

It is a formula for a society completely without balance, a pyramid at the top of which the struggle for control goes on in ever more violent and bloody fashion.

But even with a broad base of democratic government and a long tradition of freedom of choice, the "solution" in Western Europe and Britain holds out little promise. The nationalization of major industries has certainly not resolved the problem of the balance of powers in a society in which an advanced technology makes the decisions of the individual manager so important. In fact the nationalization of the railways, coal mines, and other industries seems to have added other complications—another dimension—to the problem. With a Labor or a Socialist government in power, the trade union bureaucracy is in a position to force the issue of wages and hours in the industry in which its members are employed. In other words it is difficult or impossible to arrive at terms fair in relation to other elements of the economy by a genuine bargaining process since there are no longer two sides to bargain.

In Great Britain in the years after the second world war, when a Labor government was in office, there was ample opportunity to observe what the new concentration of power meant. The propaganda in the labor movement had led the rank and file to expect that this would be the beginning of the millennium. So the demands of the unions were naturally for more of the things they had been led to believe would come with a Labor government. The bureaucracy in charge of the railways found it hard to say no. So demands were granted in this basic industry that helped to throw Britain's war-ravaged economy further out of kilter.

The attempt to bring the coal mines back to prewar production and regain Britain's markets abroad was similarly handicapped. Here the failure of private ownership had been even more glaring. The mines had not been kept up to date with the introduction of modern labor-saving machinery either out of the reinvestment of profits or from new capital investment. It was a stagnant industry using old methods and old machinery. But even with due allowances made for the failures of the past, the blurring of authority as between state and trade union was a major obstacle.

In the labor-socialist blueprint for a better world the question of the allocation of power in a planned economy had been given too little consideration. As the consequences were felt in economic and social dislocation, the Labor Party lost ground and the importance of many of the long-delayed reforms the Government put through was thereby obscured. But this must seem to anyone viewing it objectively as another instance of the hazard of trying to follow an arbitrary road map to a preconceived utopia. The lesson may be put in an even broader context with the conclusion that there is no formula for perfection that will project mankind into a self-regulating, air-conditioned Garden of Eden. So much suffering, anguish, and disillusionment have been spent in trying to find the newest model of utopia.

The continuing effort of trial and error, of building on what is and what can be, calls for so much more patience, and, what is even more important, so much more tolerance and understanding. It is the pragmatic method of trial and error that we like to think we follow here in our business society. We believe it is one of the reasons that this society has had so much success in achieving high standards of production and consumption. It is a rejection of the dogma of Marx and also of the classical liberal dogmatism. The economy is mixed, not capitalist in strict definition, and certainly not collectivist.

Yet few would argue that we have completely solved our own problem of the balance of powers that brings a healthy equilibrium and yet does not exclude the kind of tensions making for a dynamic and developing economy. On an ever smaller number of managers in big business, big labor, big government rests an ever greater share of the total authority exercised in the society. This is in large part the consequence of the kind of technology in industry and in communications that dictates ever larger and larger units for efficiency—and convenience—in production. It is also in part the consequence of the dynamic of competition. But the fact of this concentration of power creates well-nigh intolerable strains.

First of all it puts a great strain on the individual manager. The temptation to pride, to arrogance, to overweening use of unrestrained authority is ever present. It is not necessary to cite the instances in recent decades of the reckless abuse of power and the dire results not alone for the individual but for most of the rest of us. There is, however, another kind of strain that has its origins in the growing awareness of the unreal relationship between the authority of the economic unit and the authority of the political unit. The individual participates, if he is a good citizen, in the politics of his city, his county, and perhaps even his state. But decisions taken by the mayor, the city council, the county manager, the governor of the state have comparatively little bearing on the daily life of the average citizen. It is his relation to the business for which he works that conditions his whole life. About this relationship he has little or nothing to say, particularly if he is one of the many millions of Americans who work for corporations employing a thousand or more workers.

A great deal of the strain and conflict in our industrial society may be traced to this unreality. The trade union more often than not conducts a kind of internecine warfare with business management. This is carried over into politics with each group striving to gain the ascendancy so that the other can be thwarted in matters where decisions are taken by government. The anomalous relationship of the economic unit and the political unit in the exercise of power may help to explain the indifference of the average American to politics and the fact that such a small percentage of eligible voters participate even in national elections. If the daily life of the individual is governed by a management, whether of a business, a trade union, or a farm cooperative, participation in politics will seem to many an exercise in futility. Growing cynicism toward politics and politicians is one consequence.

In the "organizational revolution" the ever more pressing need, if we are to have a democratic society, is for participation of the individual to a far greater degree in a real and meaningful sense. A number of serious-minded men and women, businessmen, economists, and others have come forward with ways and means to achieve this end. It is one of the healthy signs of the times that plans and proposals, any number not only new and creative, but practical as well, are constantly being put forward.

The history of profit-sharing in its various forms illustrates the urge to participate, to work together toward a common end. Profit-sharing has in many businesses been shown to be an incentive to greater production with a larger share for each worker. In some instances profit-sharing has meant more than just an economic gain. It has brought a deeper sense of sharing in a common enterprise. But often the criticism is that profit-sharing is hardly more than another kind of bookkeeping, failing to bring with it any real sense of participation.

One of the most stimulating critics of the American economy, Peter F. Drucker, in his "The New Society," has come up with some interesting ideas on the problem of power and responsibility and the fair and democratic allocation of authority in an industrial economy. Drucker offers, as the one effective principle of social order in an advanced industrial society, participation by workers'

representatives not in the economic decisions of an industry but in the management of the plant community.
That is to say, in the management of matters of cleanli-
ness and order, routines of work and relaxation. In this
way, he believes, a mutual confidence grows up. This
must, of course, be real and not the kind of play-acting
that so-called "Junior Advisory Boards," instituted by
some companies, are plainly seen to be. Nor in Drucker's
view must the system of plant self-government be used to
thwart or harass an independent trade union. Self-government must stand on a firmer foundation than management's pleasure or it will degenerate into pure pater-
nalism and "company union."

In 1947 General Motors ran a contest on "My Job," in
which 175,000 workers entered individual essays. In two
General Motors plants, where the recreation programs
were entirely organized and run by the workers themselves, recreational activities were among the major
sources of job satisfaction, outranking even security, supervision, or pay. In contrast in plants where the recreation programs were under the control of management the
satisfaction was much smaller. According to Drucker,
there were signs of dissatisfaction, if not resentment, in
those plants where management not only sponsors but
actually runs the activities. This is true, Drucker points
out, although the company-run programs may be more
comprehensive and more generous.

One big oil company had built up a complete system
of sickness, retirement, and death benefits for its workers,
all of which were paid for by the company. An inquiry
showed, however, that the workers did not value these
benefits. In fact they felt in many instances resentment
toward the company's policies. Particularly resented was
the fact that a worker lost all his accumulated claims if
he left the company's employ or was discharged. This
seemed eminently fair to management, as the company

was paying the entire bill. To the worker that seemed a chain to hold him in the company's employ, however dissatisfied he might become.

Drucker cites the American Cast Iron Pipe Company of Birmingham, Alabama, as an example of highly successful worker self-government in the plant. At the death of the founder, who had built up the business, the workers, several thousand both white and Negro, became the owners of the capital stock twenty-five years ago. They were not particularly interested in the idea of ownership, some of them even realizing that they might have benefited more financially by a profit-sharing plan. Over the years, however, the company has developed a system of worker self-government. This has greatly strengthened the position of management, with the workers understanding that the business needs a professional managerial staff with full authority over all matters relating to the company's economic performance. They understand, according to Drucker, why this management must be paid adequate salaries. They have even come to understand why the enterprise must operate at a profit and why it is in the interests of the workers to have maximum efficiency and maximum profitability.

The author goes so far as to say that such a plant management plan can help to ease tensions not merely in a single industry but in the community itself. With a confident mutual working relationship between the trade union and management, the union would be far less likely to set out in the community to gain the kind of political control designed to frustrate management. The garment workers' unions in New York, developing a broad mutual approach with management to economic problems of the industry, have expanded their interests to cover not only the city and the state but the nation and the world.

Yet the concept of self-government of the plant com-

munity is no panacea. It is a helpful approach to the
participation of men in affairs that concern them most
immediately. If we are to have a welfare state, and
Drucker argues that it is futile to try to get rid of this
governmental structure that undertakes to satisfy man's
hopes for security, then self-government in industry becomes a necessary corollary. But let us not, he says, con-
fuse the "welfare state" with the "hand-out state."

> "If the member of society does not learn that the
> satisfaction of his hopes depends on increasing out-
> put, increasing productivity and increasing efficien-
> cy, that, in other words, it depends on *his efforts,*
> the promise of the welfare state will end in misery
> and slavery. The people will not be willing to aban-
> don their hope of security. The worse things become,
> the more they will cling to it. And they will force them-
> selves into a tyranny the sole purpose of which will
> be to enforce the equality of misery."

In many ways by the continuing process of trial and
error the effort is going forward to achieve a better balance of power, an equilibrium that means more confidence in the justice with which power is administered and
therefore greater peace of mind and enjoyment of life.
But what must never be lost sight of is that the individual is the end, the goal; the balance that he strikes within
himself, his capacity for maturity and wisdom. It is when
the individual is made the means to an end that the
whole purpose of society is subverted. He becomes a category, a perforated card in an indexing machine, a dot on
a graph.

The goal must be to release the highest potentialities
for good of each individual. If it does not do this then it
has failed. And precisely here a searching examination
of our own world today must leave us with grave doubt

as to the success or failure ultimately of the highly technological society in which we live. We must ask ourselves whether in our society the individual is achieving the only true rewards—which are peace of mind, harmony of soul, a sense of being valued for himself, of being loved and cherished because he is a child of God; whether in fact he has any real opportunity to discover such rewards.

This question arises again and again in the already cited book on "American Income and Its Use." Particularly in her analysis of the criteria of the good life in relation to how Americans actually do live, Professor Elizabeth Hoyt inquires into the ratio of contentment to the excess of material things available to us. This is not, it should be added, the familiar criticism heard in Europe and Asia that America is "materialistic." The contemporary Chinese philosopher and scholar-diplomat, Hu Shih, many years ago ridiculed the idea that the West is unspiritual because it employs modern technology to ease the tasks of daily life. The highest spiritual course, in the view of Hu Shih, is to use material goods in such a way that the potentialities of mankind for higher things are thereby released.

But whether we actually are using our great technological resources to free ourselves for adventures of the mind and spirit is the question that Professor Hoyt begs leave to ask. She suggests that we may be dominated, hag-ridden, by the very machines invented to ease the burden of living. Technology is both creator and destroyer. We are fascinated by the gadgets our civilization produces in ever greater abundance. The modern motor car is an extraordinary thing of color and glint and shine, with speed and power undreamed of twenty years ago. Yet when thousands upon thousands of those cars crowd the highways the result is more often than not a lagging pace, a welter of gasoline fumes, irritation and frustration, a toll of casualties greater than in war.

As Professor Hoyt says, technology fascinates us so much by its power over the material world that we forget that it is not all, it is not even the most important thing. It is only the means to the most important thing, which is a deeper experience of life. But the means too often becomes the end, and the end is as barren and sterile as though man had condemned himself to an endless treadmill.

One reason for the dynamic, productive quality of the American economy is modern advertising. But here particularly the confusion of ends and means is apparent. Envy and emulation are familiar tools of American advertising. They are employed with skill and subtlety to sell more things. But they do not make for greater contentment or peace of mind.

Professor Hoyt gives an estimate from the publication, *Printers' Ink,* saying that advertising in 1951 cost $6,548,-200,000. That was $42 per capita or over $150 per family. It is nearly four times the average contributed by each family to social services, including church. But, as Professor Hoyt recognizes, it is foolish to attack advertising. The root of the evil is that we have production in excess of our ability to use intelligently with the present distribution of income in the United States and the world. Advertising is one way of using up this excess and there are worse ways of using it, such as war. The emphasis should be put on wider use of our resources as a whole. And here again we come back to the fact that our productive capacities have been increased by technology out of all proportion to the degree our discrimination, appreciation, and imagination have been increased.

The advertiser must accept some responsibility for the confusion of values that is a symptom of our time of troubles. Words such as character, faith, belief, integrity, are used to commend the quality of beer and pills. If you buy a certain car you are exalted, exultant, magnificently at ease. In some instances the advertising mind is so dogmatic that any criticism brings a sharp challenge as though it were heretical even to question. Professor Hoyt says that a trade association representing national advertisers provided for the checking of textbooks and, when comments unfavorable to advertising were made, the publishers of the books were requested to approach the authors to get them to withdraw their statements. Protests were made to the presidents of colleges who had faculty members known to have held even a moderately critical view of some of the practices of advertising. In his raucous novel, "The Hucksters," Frederick Wakeman gives a picture of the advertising world so squalid, so vulgar and meretricious, that one must assume it is an unreal caricature of the less pleasant aspects of high-powered merchandising.

Now that America must accept unparalleled responsibility for keeping order in a chaotic and revolutionary world, the face that we present to other peoples becomes more important than ever before. To the outsider viewing America in the highly polished reflection of the skilled advertiser we must seem to be a people swathed in ease and luxury, complacent to the point of intolerable smugness, moving effortlessly through the years in swift motor cars, de luxe ocean liners, streamlined trains, airplanes that defy weather and space. The advertiser shows a group of Arabs staring in awed amazement at an American plane, or overcome with pleasure at the joys of an American soft drink. Thus American advertising, without being in the least aware of it, sometimes offends peoples with an ancient culture and a profoundly traditional way of life.

This is, of course, only one aspect, and in reality a minor one, of Americans living on a somewhat isolated plateau of advanced technology and high prosperity while most other peoples exist far below. The perspective, both for them and for us, is bound to be a distorted one. We can scarcely be expected to reduce appreciably our own standards of living in order to raise that of other peoples. This asks too much of human nature in its present state. As a matter of fact American generosity—enlightened self-interest may be more accurate—has gone to extraordinary length in sending billions upon billions of dollars abroad to rehabilitate war-ravaged Europe and to try to help Asians in the first painful steps along the road leading from colonialism and feudalism to independence and some of the benefits of technology. James Reston, chief Washington correspondent of the New York *Times*, returning in the fall of 1953 from a tour of Asia, reported that there were many reasons to be encouraged by the advances being made with American technicians working side by side, often under the most difficult and unhealthful conditions, with farmers and teachers in the so-called underdeveloped countries of Asia. He found that despite the gloomy, pessimistic, and critical statements of Asian leaders, made often for the purposes of internal politics and in this respect not unlike the free-wheeling statements of some of our own politicians, there was much to be hopeful about.[1]

Long before Point 4 was heard of, American teachers, businessmen, and technicians had gone out into the world to share American know-how, sometimes with profit as the motive, sometimes out of altruism and the noblest kind of idealism. Such institutions as the American College at Beirut and Athens College in Athens are one result of this deep-seated impulse. The American record in the Philippines, beginning with the determined, patient, and persistent effort of William Howard Taft to lead the Philippine people to statehood and independence, is one of which we can be justly proud.

From the high plateau of the American standard our

1 *New York Times Magazine*, Aug. 30, 1953, pp. 9 ff.

own perspective on what lies around us may come down once again to the supreme importance of balance and above all of balance in the individual. We must understand the values of societies that seem to us alien and strange. We must learn to appreciate the rewards that flow out of those values. The Hindu mystic sitting cross-legged in the dust—our favorite caricature has him on a bed of nails—may without benefit of our machine technology have entered into realms of the spirit that most of us have not even dimly perceived. Professor Hoyt makes this point with great cogency when she recalls the conditions under which the ancient Greeks lived. They walked wherever they went. Their clothes consisted of two pieces of coarse cloth held together with pins. They had no books. Their fare was coarse and simple. Yet from that simple, almost primitive society came the greatest philosophy and the greatest art in the history of the West. The harmony achieved by the Greeks has sounded across the troubled ages like the tones struck from a great bell, clear and pure and beautiful.

The paradox, as Professor Frank Knight recognized, is that the concept of individual freedom that uniquely dominates our era derives from the Middle Ages when the Christian ethic narrowly construed was enforced if necessary by torture and death. The paradox deserves more exploration by those who are increasingly concerned over the relevance of religion and ethics to daily life. From these studies the conclusion emerges that we shall achieve the redemption of ourselves and our society only by the voluntary acceptance of the brotherhood of man; by the free and ever-increasing incorporation into the very fabric of our society of the great inheritance that has come down to us out of the Greco-Judaeo-Christian tradition. An element of that inheritance is an awareness of the fact that man belongs not to himself but to God. This relationship out of that earlier era may well be the only

basis for freedom in the long run. Those who in the
short run claim a monopoly on God's truth are eager to
deny freedom to others.

There are signs that at least an awareness of the choice
before us is growing. But even when we are aware that
nothing less will suffice, nothing less than the brotherhood of man, it is difficult in the complexity of daily
living to know how to begin to relate an all-embracing
love to the decisions each of us must take in getting and
spending. This is the problem which Howard Bowen
analyzes in summarizing the goals of economic life. Individual human beings even with the noblest of intentions do not always know what is good for others, and
in any case individuals cannot be relied upon to act consistently from selfless motives. Deploring the divorce between economics and ethics, Professor Bowen undertakes
to define eleven subordinate goals—subordinate, that is, to
the ideal of love as the over-arching goal of life and therefore of economic life as well. His list of subordinate goals
—which includes fellowship, dignity and humility, en-
lightenment, esthetic enjoyment, creativity, new experience, security, freedom, and justice—will seem to some
almost hopelessly idealistic. But if the larger goal of a
good life and a good society is to be kept in view the list
can hardly be less inclusive. It is when we consider the
relation between precept and practice that we see how
far we must travel and how difficult and uncertain is the
road. Thus Professor Bowen writes:

"The degree of influence and power which the
businessman exercises over the lives of others, near
and far, places upon him the moral responsibility to
recognize the social implications of his decisions and
to consider the social interest—along with his private
interest—in arriving at these decisions. His duty is to
ask himself how the decisions he makes in the on-

going operation of his business relate to social goals and how he might advance the attainment of these goals by appropriate modification of his decisions."

This is the ideal. Yet the businessman has as his first responsibility to keep his business solvent, for if his business is bankrupt it will no longer provide a living for himself and his family and jobs for others. He may, therefore, in the course of the harsh necessity for survival during, say, a period of deflation, take decisions directly contrary to those his conscience might dictate.

Similarly the consumer might exercise a far greater degree of ethical choice in selecting from the profusion of goods and services offered on every hand. We might ask ourselves what we are getting out of all our abundant production. Does our wealth and income add up to anything important in terms of values close to the center and the meaning of life? How might the *uses* to which we devote our riches be improved? But these are questions, as Professor Bowen says, which tax our capacity to look inward, and so we turn on our television sets and ignore them. In short, we tend to consider consumption as an end in itself rather than as a means to the good life. How much of our energy and attention is given to increasing the flow of goods and services— any goods and services! And how little is given to the problem of what things are worth producing and how these might be used for the fuller attainment of deeper human purposes!

In the course of the studies conducted over the past five years the question was bound to rise again and again as to the part played by religion in the decisions the individual must take. By questionnaire and by discussion groups A. Dudley Ward directed a survey of the attitudes of Americans on a wide range of subjects. In the volume "Attitudes and Opinions of People on the American Economy" one of the startling conclusions is that religion plays little part, at least at the conscious level, in the decisions made by the thousand or more individuals included in the study. It was not that they were irreligious. Many of them were church-goers. It was simply that their religious experience did not seem to be relevant to the problems confronting them in earning their living. One gathered from their remarks that religion is something to one side, a social experience that is sometimes consoling and pleasant but one that does not strike very deep.

This anemia of the religious experience is a phenomenon that has deeply disturbed many, and particularly churchmen who are aware that they function on the periphery of the lives of even those who profess to be Christians. The significance of this pale dilution of religion in terms of the human spirit is so evident as to make comment superfluous. But considered on another and less important level it must be of deep concern to anyone who reflects on what are the sanctions underlying the surface structure of law and order. That structure can be no stronger than the acceptance of an ethic that has its roots in something deeper than the authority of the policeman and the threat of jail. The unhappy suspicion is growing that the ethical base has been disastrously eroded away in recent decades.

Thirty years ago Professor Tawney gave the first Scott Holland Memorial Lectures at Oxford. Those lectures in expanded form became "Religion and the Rise of Capitalism," which we have frequently referred to in this book. In 1949 The Reverend V. A. Demant, Regius Professor of Moral and Pastoral Theology and Canon of Christ Church, Oxford, gave another in the series of the Scott Holland Lectures. They were expanded to form the volume published three years later called "Religion and the Decline of Capitalism." It is Dr. Demant's thesis that while we became increasingly preoccupied with the internal values of our civilization we lost sight of the standards, the values, external to it. That is to say civilization, so-called, became an end in itself and not a means to the development of the deeper and meaningful values that distinguish man from beast. Capitalism presupposed social structures and above all their underpinnings inherited from the ancient and medieval world. It took for granted the solidarities and the sureties thus inherited as if they would always be there. In Dr. Demant's phrase, they were part of liberalism's unconsciousness.

On top, he says, of the organic, civic, domestic, and craft society was reared the tremendous superstructure of economic enterprise, political democracy, intellectual exploration, and technical mastery of natural forces. It never occurred to the leaders in this achievement that the foundation they were counting on might be dissipated by the very weight of the superstructure. They were, as we all are in our various situations, so excited about what they were standing for that they assumed the permanence of what they were standing on.

The extent of the erosion is difficult to estimate. Erosion may not be the right word. What has happened may perhaps be pictured more accurately if one were to imagine many of the supports taken out from under a stage on which the clash and clamor of a great drama was going forward. The supports were in this instance the highly specialized moral and social products of a peculiar historical and cultural achievement—the religious-ethical inheritance out of the Middle Ages. The actors on the stage have all too often been unaware of how the seemingly solid structure on which they stand has been undermined. It is only in the face of some terrible catastrophe, such as occurred in Germany, that we are suddenly confronted with an abyss in which we see all that was so confidently "civilized" on the brilliantly lighted stage fallen into a hell of savagery, lust, destruction, and death. What Dr. Demant finds lacking is an integrating pattern of life as a whole. There is an autonomy of science, economics, politics, education. And the question is not whether an authoritative church should take control again. It is a question whether the secular functions of society, each existing of itself and for itself, can be relied upon to serve human destiny. For many in the West the twentieth century has seemed to give quite decisively and finally a negative answer.

CHAPTER X

End or Beginning?

THE PROMISE OF AMERICA has always been twofold. On the side of abundance and well-being, the capacity to make and to increase, the promise has been fulfilled in overflowing measure. There are flaws to be sure; and, above all, flaws in the distribution of this increase in a society of free choice. But, as we have seen, even with respect to distribution great progress has been made in recent years. And we can never forget that it was the fact of America's productive strength that made it possible to destroy one tyranny and to stand up to another.

> *"Passage to India,*
> *passage, oh soul, to thee . . ."*

That was the other promise America held out to people everywhere. And it is here that the shadow of doubt has fallen darkly on what was once so radiantly bright. There is the fear both at home and abroad that we are thickening and hardening into a mold that denies the deeper and nobler promise of the new world.

The doubt has arisen partly out of fear; fear of the unknown, of the awesome responsibility for trying to keep order in a time of revolutionary upheaval. We have

seen how in this time of troubles the allegiance, the loyalties, of some Americans were weakened. And the discovery of this apostasy set up a further current of fear
and uncertainty. Demagogues have exploited these fears
with such ruthless violence as to endanger the right of
freedom, essential to the survival of a free society; for
once the right of freedom, with its corollary of voluntarily accepted responsibility, is gone, then physical survival is threatened.

We are realizing today how conformity can be enforced
by coercion, intimidation, the kind of hatred spread by
reckless demagoguery. And herd-conformity is the very
essence, the sign and symbol, of the dreadful confusion of
ends and means that is the destroying agent of our society.
As he is coerced to conform, the individual is made to
serve an end determined outside his own knowing. He is
forced to accept a stature less than that of a free human
being, and his awareness of this produces a deep and
bitter frustration.

In such ghastly visions as George Orwell's "1984" is
the ultimate end of this road. Other species than man
have achieved the perfect Communism. In the society of
the bee and the ant there is no confusion of ends and
means. Each unit serves its function or it is destroyed.

At this late date we cannot be beguiled by another New
Jerusalem. That is for the past, the easy optimism that
was inevitably followed by cynical disillusion. Justice and
freedom are not incompatible in our society. In working
toward a greater measure of justice for all, we need not
sacrifice the essential freedom of any individual. It is here
that the problem of striking a balance is most difficult as
it is also most important.

The process of thickening and hardening—the ossifica-
tion that is death—must be resisted by the individual
with all his heart and all his will. When it comes to the
organization of society, there are those who insist that it

must be all black or all white or all red. They would impose their own rigidity and inflexibility on the ever-changing pattern of human life. They would foreclose the kind of experimentation that is a sign of health in a democracy. It is in a mixed economy that is also in large measure a free economy that new forms and combinations can be tested. By such a testing process new forces come into being and they help to sustain the equilibrium of countervailing power.

This is not an easy process. It calls on the individual for unceasing effort and thought. Yet it is in such a society held in balance by freely contending powers that the opportunity for the discovery of self is open to all. There are too few among us who set out on this search. We are distracted, diverted, bewildered. But the tragic folly now would be to surrender the opportunity because the door has been so little used.

Man alone is capable of asking what he will do with his life; with the little span of time allotted to him. And likewise he can help to shape the society of which he is a part for good or ill. It is this God-given choice that sets man apart and enables him in the face of an infinite universe to call his soul his own.

To believe that he will reject this choice is to admit to utter despair. To resist the mood of pessimism, defeatism, in a time such as ours is not easy. A school of history is developing that co-relates the rise of a free society with the opening of new land to discovery and settlement that accompanied the Renaissance. Now that there is no more free land to be found, freedom itself is doomed. In other words the curtain is coming down on an era that was scarcely more than an eyewink measured on the clock of infinity.

The rationalization that accepts the end of a free society is so easy to construct. To challenge the fatalism so pleased to cry doom is more difficult. Yet there are many today who refuse to surrender to the conformity of fear and doubt; to a gloom that is as unreasoning as the facile optimism of a short time ago. They are rediscovering the inheritance so long taken for granted, the foundation so overgrown and obscured. This is no retreat into the comforting enclosure of the past. Rather it is an effort to confront man's loneliness, his fragmentation, his isolation from what has gone before. One may say, with due caution, that this is a first step, this rediscovery of the perilous place in which we find ourselves and of the confused and careless way by which we got there. In this is the beginning of hope.

Bibliography

The following is not meant to be an inclusive bibliography although it includes most of the books to which reference is made, aside from the studies carried out by a department of the National Council of Churches listed in the Foreword. There are also included books that may be helpful to those who want to go further.

ADAMS, HENRY. *Education of Henry Adams*, Houghton, Mifflin, 1935. *Mont. St. Michel and Chartres*, Houghton, Mifflin, 1937.

Addams, Jane. JUDSON, CLARA. *City Neighbor; the Story of Jane Addams*, Scribner, 1951.

ADDAMS, JANE. *Forty Years at Hull House*, Macmillan, 1935.

ALGER, HORATIO. *Struggling Upward and Other Works*, with introduction by Russell Crouse, Crown Publishers, 1945.

Antonino, St. WILLIAM T. GAUGHAN, *Social Theory of St. Antoninus from his "Summa Theologica,"* Catholic University of America, 1951.

BAER, GEORGE F. *Addresses and Writings of*, collected by his son-in-law, William N. Appel, Wickersham Press, 1916.

BERLE, ADOLPH, AND MEANS, GARDINER. *The Modern Corporation and Private Property*, Macmillan, 1937.

Blake, William. WILSON, MONA. *Life of William Blake*, R. Hart-Davis, 1948 (London).

BLAKE, WILLIAM. *Poetry and Prose of William Blake*, edited by Geoffrey Keynes, Nonesuch Press, 1927 (London).

Brandeis, Louis. DILLIARD, IRVING. *Mr. Justice Brandeis*, Modern View, 1941.

BRANDEIS, LOUIS. *Curse of Bigness*, Viking, 1934.

CALKINS, CLINCH. *Some Folks Won't Work*, Harcourt, Brace, 1937.

Calvin, John. HARKNESS, GEORGIA E. *John Calvin*, H. Holt, 1931.

Conwell, Rev. Russell. ROBERT SHACKLETON. *"Acres of Diamonds," Rev. Russell Conwell, His Life and Achievements*, Harper, 1915.

DARWIN, CHARLES. *Origin of Species*, Modern Library, 1936.

DEMANT, REV. V. A. *Religion and the Decline of Capitalism*, Scribner, 1952.

Dickens, Charles. CLARK, CUMBERLAND. *Dickens and Democracy*, C. Palmer, 1930 (London).

DISRAELI, BENJAMIN, First Lord Beaconsfield. *Sybil*, Oxford University Press, 1925.

DRUCKER, PETER P. *The New Society*, Harper, 1950.

DuPONT. *DuPont, the Autobiography of an American Enterprise*, Scribner, 1952.

Francis, St. ENGLEHART, OMER. *St. Francis of Assisi*, translated and edited by Edward Hutton, Burns, Oates, 1950 (London).

FRANKLIN, BENJAMIN. *Autobiography*, Rinehart, 1948.
GALBRAITH, KENNETH. *American Capitalism and the Concept of Countervailing Power*, Houghton, Mifflin, 1952.
Galilei, Galileo. OLIVER, PETER. *Saints of Chaos*, W. F. Payson, 1934.
GLADDEN, WASHINGTON. *Applied Christianity*, Houghton, Mifflin, 1886. *Church and Modern Life*, Houghton, Mifflin, 1908.
HAWLEY, CAMERON. *Executive Suite*, Houghton Mifflin, 1952.
HERRON, GEORGE E. *The New Redemption*, T. Y. Crowell, 1893.
Hogarth, William. MCDONALD, ROBERT M. *William Hogarth*, 1697-1764, M. A. McDonald, 1941.
Hu Shih. FORSTER, LANCELOT. *The New Culture in China*, G. Allen & Unwin, 1936 (London).
Hume, David. HEINEMANN, FRITZ. *David Hume, the Man and His Science of Man*, Hermann & Cie, 1940 (Paris).
HUME, DAVID. *Enquiry Concerning the Principles of Morals*, Clarendon Press, 1927 (Oxford).
Huxley, Thomas. AYRES, CLARENCE E. *Huxley*, W. W. Norton, 1932.
Jefferson, Thomas. ADAMS, JAMES TRUSLOW. *Jeffersonian Principles*, Little, Brown, 1928.
KAPLAN, A. D. H. AND KAHN, ALFRED E. *Big Business in a Competitive Society*, Brookings Inst., 1953.
Kelley, Florence. GOLDMARK, JOSEPHINE Co. *Impatient Crusader*, University of Illinois Press, 1953.
KEYNES, JOHN MAYNARD. *The General Theory of Employment, Interest and Money*, Harcourt, Brace, 1936.
Kingsley, Charles. BALDWIN, STANLEY E. *Charles Kingsley*, Cornell University Press, 1934.
LILIENTHAL, DAVID. *Big Business: A New Era*. Harper, 1953.
Locke, John. JAMES, DAVID G. *The Life of Reason*, Longmans, Green, 1949.
LOWRY, DR. CHARLES. *Communism and Christ*, Morehouse-Gorham, 1952.
Luther, Martin. BAINTON, ROLAND H. *Here I Stand*, Abingdon-Cokesbury Press, 1950.
Malthus, Thomas Robert. GLASS, DAVID V. *Introduction to Malthus*, Watts, 1953 (London).
Marx, Karl. BERLIN, ISAIAH. *Karl Marx, His Life and Environment*, Oxford University Press, 1948.
MARX, KARL. *Capital*, International Publishers, 1948.
MAY, HENRY F. *Protestant Churches and Industrial America*, Harper, 1949.
MAYO, ELTON. *Social Problems of an Industrial Civilization*, Routledge & K. Paul, 1949 (London).
Mill, John Stuart. STEPHEN, SIR LESLIE. *The English Utilitarians*, London School of Economics, 1950.
More, Hannah. HOPKINS, MARY ALDEN. *Hannah More and Her Circle*, Longmans, Green, 1947.
Morris, William. WILES, HECTOR V. *William Morris of Walthamstow*, Walthamstow Press, 1951 (London).

NATIONAL PLANNING ASSOCIATION. *The Five Per Cent*, 1951. *Manual of Corporate Giving*, 1952.

National Council of the Churches of Christ. TULGAR, CHESTER E. *The Case Against the National Council of Churches*, Conservative Baptist Fellowship, 1951.

NATIONAL COUNCIL OF THE CHURCHES OF CHRIST. *Christian Faith in Action*, 1951.

Oastler, Richard. DRIVER, CECIL R. *Tory Radical*, Oxford University Press, 1946.

ORWELL, GEORGE. *1984*, Harcourt, Brace, 1949.

Owen, Robert. COLE, MARGARET I. *Robert Owen of New Lanark*, Oxford University Press, 1953.

OWEN, ROBERT. *Life of Robert Owen Written by Himself*, A. A. Knopf, 1920.

PINCHOT, GIFFORD. *Breaking New Ground* (autobiography), Harcourt, Brace, 1947.

PLATO. *The Republic*, Dutton, 1950.

QUINN, THEODORE. *Giant Business*, Exposition Press, 1953.

Rauschenbusch, Walter. OXNAM, G. BROMLEY. *Personalities in Social Reform*, Abingdon-Cokesbury Press, 1950.

RAUSCHENBUSCH, WALTER. *Christianity and the Social Crisis*, Macmillan, 1910.

Roosevelt, Franklin D. ROOSEVELT, ELLIOTT. *As He Saw It*, Duell, Sloan & Pearce, 1946.

ROOSEVELT, THEODORE. *An Autobiography*, Scribner, 1920.

Rousseau, Jean-Jacques. GREEN, FREDERICK C. *Rousseau and the Idea of Progress*, Clarendon Press, 1950 (Oxford).

ROY, RALPH LORD. *Apostles of Discord*, Beacon Press, 1953.

Ruskin, John. JACKSON, HOLBROOK. *Dreamers of Dreams*, Farrar, Strauss, 1949.

————————— SCOTT, EDITH HOPE. *Ruskin's Guild of St. George*, Methuen, 1931 (London).

SAY, JEAN BAPTISTE. *Letters to Thomas Robert Malthus*, G. Harding's Bookshop, 1936 (London).

SMITH, ADAM. *An Inquiry into the Wealth of Nations*, Modern Library, 1937.

————————— *Theory of Moral Sentiments*, G. Bell & Sons, 1892.

Spencer, Herbert. KIMBALL, ELSA P. *Sociology and Education*, Columbia University Press, 1932.

TAWNEY, R. H. *Religion and the Rise of Capitalism*, A Mentor Book, Harcourt, Brace, 1952.

Taylor, Frederick Winslow. COPLEY, FRANK B. *Frederick Winslow Taylor, Father of Scientific Management*, Harper, 1923.

Temple, Archbishop William. IREMONGER, FREDERIC A. *William Temple, Archbishop of Canterbury*, Oxford University Press, 1948.

Thomas Aquinas, St. DE LA VEGA, FRANCIS JOSEPH. *Social Progress and Happiness in the Philosophy of St. Thomas Aquinas and Contemporary American Sociology*, Catholic University of America, 1949.

183

Tolstoi, Leo. BELLMAN, HAROLD. *Architects of the New Age,* S. Low, Marston & Co., 1929 (London).

TREVELYAN, GEORGE M. *Illustrated English Social History* (4 Vol.), Longmans, Green, 1949-1952.

WAKEMAN, FREDERICK. *The Hucksters,* Rinehart, 1946.

Wesley, John. BEBB, EVELYN D. *Wesley, a Man with a Concern,* Epworth Press, 1950 (London).

WHATELY, ARCHBISHOP RICHARD. *Easy Lessons on Money Matters for the Use of Young People,* J. Parker, 1845 (London).

WHYTE, WILLIAM H. JR. *Is Anybody Listening?,* Simon and Shuster, 1952.

Wilberforce, William. MCCONNELL, FRANCIS T. *Evangelicals, Revolutionists and Idealists,* Abingdon-Cokesbury Press, 1942.

Wilson, Woodrow. BAKER, RAY STANNARD. *Woodrow Wilson,* Scribner, 1946.

WOYTINSKY, PROF. W. S. AND ASSOCIATES. *Employment and Wages in the United States,* 20th Century Fund, 1953.

Index of Names

A

Abrams, Frank, quoted, 90; 95
Adams, Henry, cited, 16
Addams, Jane, 77
Agee, James, quoted, 153
Alger, Horatio, 80
Allen, Frederick Lewis, quoted, 121-122
American Cast Iron Pipe Co., 165
American Council of Christian Laymen, 155
American Council of Churches, 154
American Tel. & Tel. Co., 92, 97
Antoninus, St., cited, 12
Aquinas, Thomas, quoted, 12
"A & P," 108

B

Baer, George F., quoted, 86
Baldwin, Stanley, 158
Bassett, H. Y., quoted, 93
Bastiat, Frédéric, quoted, 41
Beecher, Henry Ward, cited, 70; quoted, 137, 140
Bennett, John C., cited, 31, 147; quoted, 19
Benson, Ezra T., quoted, 120
Berle, Adolf A., cited, 104, 105
Bilsland, Lord, quoted, 116
Blake, William, quoted, 49, 114
Bloom, Clark C., cited, 42
Boulding, Kenneth, cited, 13, 37, 55, 62, 73, 74, 112-6; quoted, 36-7
Bowen, Howard R., cited, 43, 77, 98, 99; quoted, 172-3

Bradford, William, cited, 30
Brandeis, Louis, quoted, 106-7
Brownell, Herbert, quoted, 105
Buckham, J. W., quoted, 146
Bureau of Mines, U. S., 119
Bushnell, Horace, quoted, 138

C

Calumet & Hecla Company, 93
Calvin, John, 28-31; quoted, 29
Carey, Henry, 41, 42
Carnegie Steel Corporation, 139
Celler, Emanuel, 104
Chartists, The, 59-60
Chaplin, Charlie, 92
Chase National Bank, 97
Chickering, Jonas, quoted, 85
Christian Advocate, The, quoted, 140
Church of England, 59, 60
Clark, John Maurice, cited, 39
Community Chests, 94
Congregationalist, The, quoted, 140
Conwell, Russell, quoted, 137

D

Darwin, Charles, 64, 65, 69, 77
Demant, V. A., cited, 174-6
de Coincy, Gautier, quoted, 20
Dickens, Charles, 45
Disraeli, Benjamin, 45
Doddridge, Philip, 56
Donne, John, quoted, 132
Drucker, Peter F., cited, 163-6; quoted, 166
DuPont Company, 87

Index of Subjects

166-7, 171; of enterprise, 48, 76, 77, 79, 103, 104; sources of, 171-172, 178

G

Government, intervention in economic life, 11-12, 18, 24, 29, 30, 32, 35, 39, 41, 43, 44, 47, 48, 68-9, 97, 98, 99, 104, 105, 106, 108, 110, 111, 117-135, 157, 161, 162, 163, 166, 179

I

Imperialism, 23, 25
Incentives, 18, 81, 87, 88, 92, 96, 98, 100, 118, 119
Individualism, 15, 16, 18, 26, 42, 43, 44, 46, 47, 48, 116, 151, 152, 156
Investment, 23, 32, 34, 37, 122, 124-5, 127, 159, 161

J

Justice, 46, 47, 58, 61, 68, 69, 96, 134, 143, 145, 148, 151, 153, 166, 172, 178

L

Labor, conditions of, 13, 20, 21, 38, 39, 41, 44, 45, 49, 51, 57-60, 77, 92, 107, 140-141, 149, 160, 163, 164; conflicts, 136, 139-140, 141, 158, 162; division of, 13, 34-35, 36-7, 40; participation in management, 160, 162-6; unions, 58, 60, 110, 111, 112, 113 ff., 128, 149, 160, 161
Laissez faire, 16, 19, 34 ff., 41, 43, 44, 48, 49, 66, 77, 86, 99, 117-120, 130, 134, 150
Liberty, 36, 39, 46, 47, 48, 75, 107, 155. *See also* Freedom
Love, as value, *see* Altruism

M

Management, 90-100, 107-8, 162-6
Manufacturing, 45, 49, 50, 56, 102, 103, 125, 126
Market, free, 119, 120; mechanism of, 38, 41, 42, 43
Materialism, 13, 16, 22, 30, 32-3, 73, 76, 137-8, 167
"Mixed economy," 133, 135, 161
Monopoly, 21, 30, 61, 159

N

Neo-orthodoxy, 148
Neurosis, 81-2
"New Deal," 82, 87, 123

O

Organization, church, 11-14, 16, 17, 29-30, 35; ethical aspects of, 112-6; other groups, 18, 35, 94, 106, 108, 112-6; social, 15, 17, 21, 23, 25, 36. *See also* Community, Corporations, Labor

P

Planning, economic, 119, 161
Pluralism, 36, 40, 77, 179
Poverty, 13, 20, 21, 36, 45, 49, 50, 79-80, 131, 151, 171
Power, 15, 38, 55, 86, 89, 90
Predestination, 31, 64
Prices, constituents of, 35; control of, 14, 21, 22, 30, 109, 134; fixed, 13, 21, 22, 30; fluctuation of, 133; noncompetitive, 108, 109, 111; reduction of, 88-9, 159; revolution in, 23
Productivity, 13, 34, 37, 38, 42, 88, 89, 92, 108, 109, 125, 130, 132, 159